Jackie Reardon

Hans Dekkers

MINDSET

Translated from the Dutch
by Beverley Jackson

MINDSET PUBLISHERS

Thank you for buying this book. The proceeds will go to the
Mindset Foundation which supports young South African
women to further their education.
www.foundation.themindset.eu

This book is published by
Mindset Publishers
Nieuwe Leliestraat 27 huis
1015 SJ Amsterdam
www.themindset.eu

Translated from the Dutch by Beverley Jackson – www.jacksonacademic.nl
Graphic design by Aart Jan Bergshoeff – www.aartjan.nl

Cover designed by hgpdesign, Alphen aan den Rijn

ISBN 978 90 4391 256 3

CONTENT

Foreword by Stanley Franker   5

Mindset as an adventure   7

Mindset in a nutshell   11

Chapter 1: The malfunctioning machine and mindfulness   19

Pillar 1: Friendly eyes   24

Pillar 2: Good mistakes   25

Intermezzo 1: Mindset in practice: a mental warming up   34

Chapter 2: It's your game   37

Pillar 3: Curiosity   38

Pillar 4: Self-knowledge   43

Intermezzo 2: Choosing a good coach   54

Chapter 3: Playing tennis with a beard   57

Pillar 5: Self-discipline   61

Intermezzo 3: Is this cheating? And how to deal with bad calls?   68

Chapter 4: Life versus sport   73

Pillar 6: Acceptance   80

Chapter 5: Action thinking: the art of concentration   85

Chapter 6: Story thinking: how do you escape from it? *101*

Intermezzo 4: Improving your technique through feeling *116*

Chapter 7: Tactics are based on feeling *119*

Intermezzo 5: Passion *134*

Chapter 8: Odysseus and the Lotus-Eaters *137*

Intermezzo 6: Mindset at its best *147*

 Mindmaps *148*

Chapter 9: Personal success plan for action thinking (PSP) *151*

 A story to end with *171*
 Epilogue by Jackie Reardon *173*
 Epilogue by Hans Dekkers *176*
 Acknowledgements *179*
 Recommended reading *181*
 Index *182*
 Notes *184*

FOREWORD BY STANLEY FRANKER

The mental part of the game is by far the most crucial. We all know that this aspect has been terribly neglected. The book Mindset offers exercises as a tool to consciously experience what is going on between one's ears during practice and competition. Through the six pillars, the basis of the Mindset method, one is enabled to experience what is exactly going on in one's mind. The six pillars can be used as a compass to keep you focused. According to this method once you have the program right, you can't get lost in your own mind again. As a matter of fact you will be in total control of yourself both in training sessions as in matches.

Verify your mindset, your commitment to excellence and find out what the content of the book is adding up to. It is imperative that you approach the book with an open mind. Most of the time you get out of something what you put into it. Nothing comes easy unless you're passionately involved.

Mastering these skills will also be beneficial to you in other endeavors. With the help of this book one will stay focused because of the right mindset and therefore reach any goal you choose.

J. Stan Franker MA
Stanley Franker (born 1945 in Paramaribo, Suriname); studied social psychology at the University of Southern California with a Masters in Physical Education. Former driving force of the Austrian Davis Cup team, where he helped Thomas Muster develop his game. From 1986 to 1998 Stanley was Technical Director of the Dutch Tennis Federation and captain of the Netherlands Davis Cup team and led the team, with players such as Richard Krajicek, Paul Haarhuis, Jacco Eltingh and Jan Siemerink, from the European Zone to the World Group.

MINDSET AS AN ADVENTURE

This book is intended for sports people and coaches of all levels. Reading this book is like going on an adventure. The adventure consists of finding a different way of dealing with the mental side of sport. We hope and believe that a real adventurer will become a better player and gain more enjoyment from time spent on the sports field after reading this book. Step by step, we aim to help you gain more insight into your game. We want to teach you to exploit your positive qualities and to recognize and change your negative sides, whether you are a beginner or a professional sportsman or sportswoman, a club coach or someone who coaches professionals. What we hope to achieve is that even in a difficult match or a demanding training session, you will get a kick out of your new-found ability to relax and concentrate at the same time, and to get the best out of yourself.

Why is this book called *Mindset*? A 'mindset' is a way of thinking. A mentally strong player has a particular way of thinking, which we call 'action thinking'. We refer to the opposite way of thinking as 'story thinking'. This book explains how story thinking can be changed into action thinking.

More and more players now realize the overriding importance of the mental side of sport, and know that you can improve your game immensely by working on it. Dwelling too long on your mistakes, focusing too much on the score, playing against yourself: everyone knows that these things happen during matches, causing you to tense up and make unnecessary mistakes. Of course technique is an indispensable part of the game at every level, but our emphasis here is on the mental side of sport rather than technique. The understanding you can gain here can certainly be used while you are working on improving your technique: you can learn to make the improvements you want in an enjoyable way.

You do this by changing the habit patterns of your mind. We shall give you tools that will help you to set about improving and strengthening your mental powers. The key is to invest instead of to consume. If things are not going smoothly, trying to solve the problem by going off to take a few extra lessons is a form of consumerism that can have the opposite effect. You can't expect a few hours of coaching to produce results without actively investing in your own plan for mental development.

Mindset will teach you how to conquer your fears and to calm your thoughts, using action thinking. In the tension of a match (or in the stress of everyday life) you may often find that you lose the sense of ease with which you perform to the best of your ability. Deploying the right instruments can evoke action thinking. During the game itself, scanning and zooming (observation) take over, and thoughts become subordinate to feelings (bodily awareness). We shall be basing ourselves here on the scientific work of Robert Nideffer to clarify this process. In our view, all thoughts should be disengaged once the action in the match has begun. Decisions should be taken instinctively. This may sound exaggerated or even peculiar, but if we listen to what leading sports personalities say about a 'flow', it always comes down to the same thing: 'I didn't think, I acted.' *Mindset enhances instinct.*

Mindset has developed a vocabulary that is concrete, simple, modern and accessible. It is 'accessible' in the sense that the terminology is neutral/ objective rather than confrontational. Take this example. A coach saying to a pupil that he is 'in story thinking' will have a very different impact from saying that his play is far too tense. We have seen in practice that this makes a world of difference. In fact we have even heard pupils of different sports telling each other that they were 'in story thinking', without any of the depressing, frustrating overtones that usually accompany such situations. In other words, this terminology tends to motivate people instead of making them feel hurt or put down.

And since the vocabulary is simple, it soon becomes clear where the work has to be done. It also gives the pupil more insight into his or her own responsibility. Better self-management gives people the energy they need to make changes.

Mindset provides sports coaches with a general framework for communicating with their pupils, using one or two words instead of complex sentences. This makes it possible to communicate about the mental side of the game in a specific and tangible manner.

In this book, our philosophy is applied to sport. But the two mindsets, story thinking versus action thinking, can be applied to any activity, using sport as a metaphor.

Consider, for a moment, the different ways in which someone may make music. The story thinker plays notes. Technically, everything may be perfect, but there is not the slightest bit of feeling in the way he plays. The action thinker interprets. For him, the notes are just a basis to go on. 'That was played with great feeling' is a comment that has nothing to do with story thinking and everything to do with action thinking.

The same applies to communication. Sometimes you may fill in all the gaps yourself when someone is trying to tell you something. What you hear fits precisely into the image that you already had of the person. This is the story-thinker's judgment. It may turn out to be very surprising if you listen with more empathy and try, without making any judgement, to understand the real motives behind the person's words. You may suddenly realize that you've never listened to him or her properly before, with the action thinker's attention, but were already thinking up your own story or answer while he was still speaking.

We do not claim that our approach is the one and only way of achieving your potential in sport. Many roads lead to Rome. We are convinced, however, that everyone who adopts an open mind to our approach can benefit from it and become a more complete sportsman. The inspiration for this book was drawn from over a hundred tennis holidays in the past eighteen years, the insight training of S.N. Goenka ('Vipassana'), The Seven Habits by Stephen R. Covey and the books of Eckhart Tolle. These were the signposts that helped to keep us on course. Another source of inspiration was 'The Power of Full Engagement' by Jim Loehr and Tony Schwartz. Their ideas and approach helped to shape our ideas for the personal success plan (PSP), which at the end of this book will help you choose a single mental goal that is most relevant to you   .

Our method is not based on scientific research, although numerous academic studies and sports psychologists support our approach. What matters to us is that we have received positive feedback not only from academic circles but also, and most notably, from the world of professional sport. Mindset has been officially integrated into the training system of the Dutch tennis federation, and a great many professional coaches in a wide range of sports have praised the practical usefulness and accessibility of the Mindset method. Now that the book is available in an English translation, we are also receiving a growing stream of enthusiastic reactions from countries around the world. We have been flooded with e-mails from recreational players saying that they have made amazing progress since applying the Mindset principles. For years now, Mindset training sessions have been producing immediate and astonishing results.

MINDSET IN A NUTS

OUR PHILOSOPHY

All around us, there are signs of a movement away from the lifestyle and way of thinking that are associated with the rat race towards a more conscious way of living and thinking. Mindfulness, slowing down the pace of life and stress management are all terms that no longer sound vague or esoteric. We call the traditional mentality of judging, rationalizing and attachment to the past and the future 'story thinking'. The new way of thinking that *Mindset* advocates is governed by observing non-judgmentally, visualizing and focusing on the here and now. We call this balanced mindset 'action thinking'.

By changing your mindset, you will get the best out of yourself, and you will find yourself able to do far more than before with the same level of skill. Getting into a flow is within anyone's reach, provided you know what to focus on. *Mindset* is a mental guide that teaches you to change from story thinking into action thinking. You will learn how to be in the here and now, and to conquer the interference coming from the ego. Winning from yourself will become more important than winning from your opponent. Once you have mastered this way of thinking, you will always be able to give your best performance.

Someone who could serve as a good role model to everyone in this respect is Roger Federer. He says that in the course of his career he has increasingly learned how to relax and how to play one point at a time. He states quite literally that he finds it more important to outperform himself than his opponents. Other sportsmen in whom he recognizes the same mentality include the golf legend Tiger Woods, the amazing tennis icon Pete Sampras and the Formula One racing driver Michael Schumacher.

cases, their success comes from a constant drive to perform at er level rather than to win from an opponent. They have learned to prove their own concentration to a level at which their achievements derive almost entirely from action thinking rather than story thinking. It hardly needs to be added that it is also their natural talent, self-discipline and determination that have made them better than the rest.

In general we tend to resist change, because our usual patterns feel comfortable; changing patterns requires energy and effort, and is sometimes painful. We are always searching for excuses to avoid change. The only way of changing old patterns into new ones is through practice and repetition. Every day you practise means progress. This is an essential element of the Mindset philosophy. Shifting from story to action thinking does not mean that we have to turn our thoughts off altogether, it means finding new patterns to help us switch off the 'noise' of story thinking. Only then can we learn how to focus to the best of our ability. This book does not pay much attention to technique or tactics, but strangely enough, everyone who reads it will discover that they make progress in both these areas. The explanation for this is that the mental side of sport is simply the overriding factor.

In story thinking, there is a big difference between winning and losing; the result is quite obviously either one or the other. Action thinking makes it possible to win every time. If you are bogged down in story thinking, you have simply won or lost, in sports terms, according to the scoreboard. In action thinking you can win twice: from yourself, and in addition, sometimes from your opponent too. You win from yourself if you set realistic goals for yourself beforehand, in a match as well as in a training session, and achieve them by carrying out your plan consistently and with discipline. You will learn to experience this as a victory. Eventually you will start to realize that winning from yourself is more important than winning from your opponent. And with this attitude will come a new feeling of self-confidence.

'My only goal is to win this match.' This is something you will hear sports people of all levels say more frequently than almost anything else. And the funny thing about this statement is that it essentially has no content at all. This winning does not serve any goal, no specific plan has been mapped out that can be worked on, it does not provide any guidelines as to what you hope to achieve, and all it does is add tension. Bettine Vriesekoop (twice European table-tennis champion) wrote the following comment in response to the first edition of *Mindset*: 'If you think in terms of winning or losing you're always in a position of dependency. If you give quality to all your actions, the results will come by themselves.'

Mindset is not about learning a few useful tips, although there will be a few of those along the way. It is about something much more important. It is about changing our whole way of thinking about sport and about ourselves.

FEELING (BODILY AWARENESS)

The magic word that will enable you to discard story thinking and shift to action thinking is feeling. The method explained in *Mindset* will teach you exactly what this feeling is: a concentration form based on bodily awareness, and how you can use it to change.

One of the most familiar sporting experiences, something that everyone has felt from time to time, is tensing up and choking. You try desperately to remain light-footed, but stay rooted to the spot. A growing sense of confusion sets in; you have no idea what you should do with the ball. Thoughts keep flashing through your mind. This is the story thinker. An action thinker activates himself by using trigger-words, breathing techniques and rituals. This shifts his focus to the visual, without thoughts intervening and paralyzing him.

The methods briefly referred to above are a few of the instruments that will enable you to shift from thoughts to the feelings that go with action thinking. Everyone will recognize these tools, but very few find them easy to apply. People are constantly surprised that negative emotions keep getting in the way. And they have no idea what to do about it, what sort of training might be useful. Even Federer used to have trouble with his emotions.

According to Federer, finding a way to calm his mind has been of crucial importance to his career. He used to experience his matches as a series of emotional peaks and valleys. Each one completely exhausted him. Whenever he won two matches, he knew he was bound to lose the next.

'I had to learn how to relax', says Federer. 'Instead of going through a constant emotional roller-coaster, I had to stay calm. Play one point at a time. Concentrate on the ball. Since I have learnt how to do that, my career has taken off amazingly. These days I feel just as relaxed on as off court. I also enjoy playing much more'.
Roger Federer after winning his third US Open title (The People's Daily, September 12, 2006)

We cannot emphasize enough that 'achieving the right feeling' is a process that cannot be evoked simply by using a few devices on the sports field (with instruments such as visualization, trigger-words, breathing and rituals). The learning process begins elsewhere. It is only when you have achieved a change in mindset that the 'instruments' that can be deployed during a match can be really effective and enable you to shift into action thinking. In other words, if you want to achieve the right feeling during sport, you have to lay the foundations in everyday life. That is the essence of the personal success plan that is presented for you to use in chapter 9. There are no quick, short-term solutions although you will notice immediate results. Mental growth is a process of consciousness-raising. The foundations on which you can build this growth are the six pillars, the four concentration forms and the nine instruments.

OUR METHOD – AN OVERVIEW

The aim of Mindset is to provide a method that will enable people to develop mental resilience both in matches and in other situations. The method aims at consciousness-raising, with the ultimate aim of acting unconsciously. Eventually you learn to act on the basis of feeling and intuition.

The basic conditions that are mentioned below are the six pillars that underpin our method. We regard these six pillars as universally applicable.

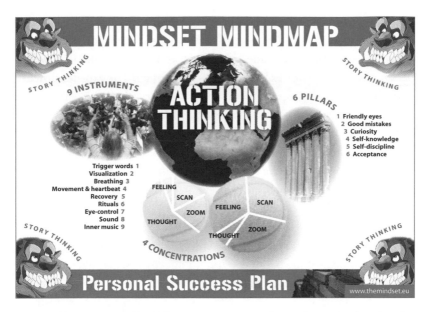

We shall return to all of them many times throughout the book. The Mindset Mindmap above will also be clarified throughout the book.

Personal development can make or break progress in sport. There is growing appreciation today for the fact that personal development in other areas of life is crucial to improving your mental powers in your chosen sport.

THE SIX PILLARS

1. Friendly eyes
2. Good mistakes
3. Curiosity
4. Self-knowledge
5. Self-discipline
6. Acceptance

1. Friendly eyes

Friendly eyes and good mistakes are the two most important 'pillars' on which to base your development as an action thinker. They are the foundation of achieving a balanced mind: action thinking. If you look with friendly eyes, objectively and non-judgmentally – not just at yourself but also at the world around you – emotions will lose their power over you. This will make you less vulnerable, since you will not take everything personally. Here is an example: 'If my opponent tries to disrupt my game with intimidating comments or behaviour, I shall not get irritated or see it as a personal attack. I will not let it influence me. In fact I can even understand why he or she might act that way.' Another example: 'If I get furious with myself for playing way below my standard, I will understand that I am doing the best I can at this given moment.'

'Friendly eyes' is a state of mind that every sportsman should pursue.

2. Good mistakes

If you boldly pursue a specific goal, you may not succeed straight away. In fact it would be quite odd if you did not make a few mistakes along the way, before you succeed in making a change successful and permanent. If someone walks off the court or field in disappointment after losing a match, he may deal with the defeat in two different ways. He can learn from what happened, seeing the match as a 'good mistake'. He can re-mind himself that progress is not always immediately visible and carry on optimistically down the path of personal development. Or he can look at the defeat as a personal disaster, which will close off ways of learning from it and make progress impossible. 'Good mistakes' is a way of reasoning that makes every situation a learning experience.

3. Curiosity

If you are curious about how you behave on and off the sports field, you will gather information to help you enhance your performance. This curiosity may be about how you are playing, and how your opponent is playing, but also about the emotions that come to the surface. Self-management begins with curiosity, and this includes open questions. For example asking your coach: 'What do you think the best way is for me to improve mentally?' The brain can be trained, just like a muscle. So curiosity is very valuable, since it leads to new discoveries that can help you to make changes. Once you realize this, there is no longer any such thing as failure. 'Good' and 'bad' become meaningless concepts: there is just scope for growth. Curiosity leads to self-knowledge.

4. Self-knowledge

Self-knowledge grows through shared knowledge. Self-knowledge does not only come from solitary reflection; more importantly, it comes from asking for open, honest feedback, for instance from your coach or teammates. Self-knowledge will always remain limited if you are not open to the opinions of others.

Self-knowledge is an essential part of setting goals, since you need to know what is within your own capabilities. Everyone who is involved in sport needs to set a mental goal as well as setting goals in technique, tactics and fitness. It is crucial to choose a goal that is specific and achievable. What exactly are you demanding of yourself, why, and how are you going to go about it? From this situation you can really start changing things to your advantage.

5. Self-discipline

Letting go of old patterns creates space for change. Deploying new patterns calls for self-discipline, for which patience is absolutely essential. We all realize this, but how do we muster the energy to remain disciplined when the going gets tough? Reflecting on a daily basis about what you want to change and what your long and short term goals are, will motivate you to carry on. Realising what value this change will bring can make self-discipline a pleasure. We feel the need to emphasize that self-discipline is the only real discipline. The sportsman needs to find the fire from within himself, only then can a real change take place. The fact that you are doing everything that is within your power, gives you the fuel to continue and produces the beginnings of acceptance.

6. Acceptance

Once you are aware of what you need to work on and accept this, there will be more space to focus on your strengths. You can use your energy to focus on the positive instead of fighting the negative. This generates a sense of calm, as a result of which your self-confidence will grow. You will be more appreciative of your efforts, which will diminish frustrations and fears and increase your enjoyment. Your self-respect too will be boosted. This will improve your performance and make you into a more balanced player.

THE FOUR CONCENTRATIONS
(ATTENTION CONTROL)

Only once the athlete has understood the concepts of the six pillars, will he be able to work efficiently on the four concentrations (attention control). Concentration is the most important aspect of all sports, but if this is not combined with a balanced mind (six pillars) it can never be 'purely' trained as the mind keeps getting in the way of focus. There are four forms of concentration, scan, zoom, feeling and thought. Feeling is supported by the nine instruments. This will all be clarified in chapter 5 and 6. It is enough to say for this moment that a balanced mind is needed to be able to concentrate. Concentration and a balanced mind are therefore inseparable. These are the two wings that make a bird fly. If one of them does not work the bird cannot fly.

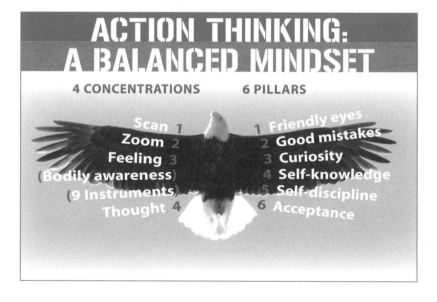

ACTION THINKING:
A BALANCED MINDSET

4 CONCENTRATIONS   6 PILLARS

Scan 1   1 Friendly eyes
Zoom 2   2 Good mistakes
Feeling 3   3 Curiosity
(Bodily awareness)   4 Self-knowledge
(9 Instruments)   5 Self-discipline
Thought 4   6 Acceptance

CHAPTER 1

THE MALFUNCTIONING MACHINE AND MINDFULNESS

CHANGING YOUR MINDSET

This chapter explains why your technique will improve more rapidly if you make attitude your priority.

Who would not want to achieve this?

1. To play freely during a match situation instead of tensing up.
2. Not to have to fight against yourself during a match.
3. To feel acceptance and self-confidence instead of frustration about your game.
4. Not to feel irritated by your opponent.
5. To gain insight into your talents and limitations.
6. To transform your fear of failure into faith in yourself and self-confidence.
7. To know how best to focus/concentrate, both in training sessions and in matches.
8. To change the 'battlefield' feeling into a 'playing field' feeling.

In our lives, we are constantly consuming things: food, goods, culture. We do it all the time. All these things change us. And yet we are reluctant to spend time on the most valuable thing in our lives: our mind. Every aspect of our behaviour is determined by our thoughts. Our mindset determines our emotions, and influences our actions and our attitude. Why don't we try to change our mindset, if that will enhance the quality of our lives and improve the way we play our sport?

Psychological processes are all-important in sport. Driven by the urge to learn, players will not only improve their sporting discipline, but also gain a better understanding of their actions on and outside of the sporting arena. The reader will go through a plan, in stages, which will set him on the path to self-knowledge and a realistic self-image. It would surely give everyone a sense of relief to learn to regard what we call 'failure' – which can have such a devastating effect in our achievement-oriented society – as a totally absurd concept.

Coaches and players of all levels often find themselves facing the same problem. They have spent years working on their technique, tactics and fitness, and it has become clear on both sides (that is, to pupils and coach alike) that they have almost reached a certain 'ceiling'. But here is some good news. You can always carry on developing the mental side of your game, and you can even do so when you are not on the sports field at all. It will not only provide a new impulse to your game, but it will also give you the motivation that can lead to a more harmonious cooperation between players and coach.

If you don't work on improving, you may lose your self-confidence and your self-respect. Failure exists only if you do nothing. If a certain achievement has eluded us, we may easily regard this as a failure. What we fear most is failure in the eyes of others, more than failure in our own eyes. If we are honest with ourselves, this is what often happens in the sporting arena. Everyone can see us failing; that is even more shattering than in everyday life! That is why emotions in sport are often almost impossible to control or to understand. Feelings like despair, shame, false pride or agitation may take hold of us. They may paralyze us and make us unsure of ourselves. As soon as we see that we can't fail as long as we set realistic goals and work towards them, our self-confidence will grow and we will enjoy ourselves far more, on and off court.

If you are having trouble with your game during a match, you can do one of two things: ignore it or work on it. Only in the latter case will you enjoy yourself, although the changes you make may sometimes be diffi-cult. You realize that you have accepted a challenge. That implies growth. Accepting the risk of failure is also growth. Passivity leads to frustration and a loss of self-confidence. Constantly trying to learn, sometimes fail-ing and sometimes succeeding, trying again and again – that will always work much better than doing nothing and waiting to see what happens.

Change your attitude by adopting a new mindset

This book is about changing the way we think about sport and about ourselves. A new mindset, or to use a more philosophical term, a new paradigm. A paradigm is a conceptual framework, a frame of reference, a way of thinking. The most famous paradigm shift is probably the one that Copernicus caused when he stated that the earth rotates around the sun, instead of the other way round. This changed our perceptions not only of the universe, but also of our place as human beings in that universe. The earth was no longer at the centre. Although this book does not deal with revolutionary change on this global scale, within our modest context of the sporting arena we are in fact discussing a dramatic change in attitude. As we have explained, it has to do with changing from story thinking to action thinking. 'Malfunctioning machine' and 'mindfulness' are metaphors we use to clarify this change.

It is common to find athletes practising the same technique over and over again, in the solemn belief that 'practice makes perfect'. This repetition is essential, they believe, to attain a higher level. But endlessly repeating the wrong technique is obviously pointless. It will only lead to frustration. In fact, while good practice helps to create good habits, bad practice helps to create bad habits. And frame of mind is an essential part of good practice. To introduce a specific change in technique with precision and finesse requires the right kind of concentration.

We cannot emphasize enough that the mental side of your game needs highly regular training in exactly the same way as technique and fitness. To strengthen a muscle, you have to train it again and again. The same applies to technique and fitness. This process is never 'finished', and the same applies to training mental processes. If you read this book and then assume that you have now got the hang of this mental stuff, that would be an illusion. Training your mental responses calls for a sustained effort (and relaxation, just as when training muscles!) and is a constant process. But it is also true that a challenging physical workout is just as essential as a challenging mental workout, since you can never change story thinking purely through mental activity. The mental and physical aspects of life are inextricably linked. You can only get into action thinking by translating mental training into physical activity.

The malfunctioning machine = story thinking

People want to learn a sport, so they take lessons, where they generally try to learn as much technique as possible. After a while they think they have learned enough to be able to play a match, and sign up for a tournament. Then, if they do less well than expected, they blame their technique and ask their coach to work on their weak points. Although they have noticed that they did much better during training sessions than in matches, they still focus all their energy on improving technique. This process can carry on indefinitely, even when they have reached a reasonably high standard. They constantly complain about their achievements in matches and express surprise that they almost always play 'below their level' in tournaments. Within this mindset, technique is simply an instrument for attaining a single goal: winning matches. In adopting this approach, the player is unconsciously making himself a slave of the 'machine' – the machine that is supposed to be providing the right technique. It is not the player but the machine that is responsible. If the machine breaks down, the player fails. If that happens, the only solution is to take the machine to the coach, who has to fix it. You often hear players who have lost a match making remarks like, 'It was simply because my backhand wouldn't work'. The sad thing is that this way of thinking guarantees that the machine will never achieve its optimum capacity and the player will always be dissatisfied. The machine is never good enough.

Mindfulness = action thinking

Mindfulness involves a completely different approach. In this way of thinking, technique is still very important of course, but it is not the beginning and end of the story. The beginning and end of this mindset is self-knowledge. If people become conscious of the fact that their 'bad' and 'frustrating' play is caused primarily not by problems of technique, tactics or fitness, but by mental factors, they finally start asking themselves the really important question: how can I improve the mental side of my game?

This may all sound rather abstract, and perhaps the reader is thinking: 'What in heaven's name has all this got to do with sport?' But by finding out ways in which you can direct your mental responses more efficiently, you will start to experience more energy and enjoyment on the sports field.

Those who give up their focus on the 'malfunctioning machine' and switch to an approach based on mindfulness will achieve greater satisfaction in their chosen sport and in other areas of life.

Action thinking and story thinking in the spirit of Jung

Every human being has a light side (action thinking) and a shadow side (story thinking). The famous psychologist Carl Jung called the dark side of the human psyche the Shadow: everything we are but do not want to be. According to Jung, the Shadow is an unconscious obstacle that can frustrate even our best intentions. Since it is an unconscious obstacle, it is vital to become familiar with this dark side, in order to deal with it and to modify it into what we do want to be. It is extremely difficult to eliminate the dark side altogether. What we can do, however, is to learn how to deal with it by becoming conscious of it. Exactly the same applies to the way in which we focus our concentration during a match. In sport too, it will be a challenge to change our Shadow into a positive experience of the 'Light side'. We first have to become conscious of the Shadow. It is only when we have taken that step (from unconscious incompetence to conscious incompetence) that we can start changing all that negative energy that poisons our concentration into a staged development in the direction of ideal concentration. Even professional players struggle with it in every match. Sometimes people are baffled by the fact that players who have had so much experience and so much coaching still struggle with concentration problems. The answer is easy: the Shadow constantly rears its head. Again and again you find yourself having to do battle with it. Just as you have to practise your technique thousands of times to perfect it, you constantly have to do battle to achieve the right kind of concentration. Don't let this discourage you. It is a challenge. Just as you can eventually learn to hit a great topspin backhand by practising it endlessly, you can also improve your concentration by working hard at it.

Who is your toughest opponent?

Your toughest opponent is usually yourself. In matches, you will more often be playing against yourself than against your opponent. Frustration and a sense of powerlessness do not come from your opponent but are caused by yourself. So self-management is crucial. What do you have the power to influence, and what is beyond your influence? With this knowledge, you can become a balanced player, someone who knows how to train with enjoyment and a sense of well-being. The clearer and more specific your self-management is, the likelier you are to succeed.

Uncertainty is the only certainty you have. In all sports, uncertainty is an essential part of the game. It is learning how to deal with this uncertainty that makes sport so fascinating and challenging. Just imagine that you always knew beforehand exactly how your match was going to be played! That would eventually ruin all your pleasure and motivation.

'Friendly eyes' are a key part of action thinking. Friendly eyes and good mistakes are the first two pillars on which to base your development as an action thinker. They are the foundations of the Mindset method.

PILLAR 1: FRIENDLY EYES

In our view, what stops us looking with friendly eyes is the dominant role of value judgments in our society. Instead of looking at yourself and the world around you judgmentally, you could try looking as an observer. Without immediately judging the way either you or your opponent is playing, you could try to observe both actions as objectively as possible.

Looking with 'friendly eyes' doesn't mean glossing over your mistakes and resigning yourself to your shortcomings. It means knowing how to neutralize your emotions at the appropriate time so that they cannot disrupt your equilibrium. This will help you to conserve energy so as to focus on the things that matter. If Zidane had reacted neutrally to Materazzi's comment in the 2006 World Cup Final, France might well have won the championship. In any case, Zidane could have bowed out of his soccer career with a greater sense of satisfaction. Especially when your opponent tries to provoke you or behaves obnoxiously, focusing on 'friendly eyes' will help you to focus on what is expected of you in the match. This will be a valuable asset.

Over the years, it has struck us that players watching a video of their matches often focus only on the negative things. On tennis holidays we often hear people say things like 'Ugh, I look so stiff! (or awkward, slow, unathletic)' or 'Pfff, I'm playing so badly!' People just starting up as professional players do not react very differently. Their eyes ('unfriendly eyes') can only see their shortcomings and mistakes. If they have made progress recently, they do not recognise it and it doesn't even interest them. Most players seem almost incapable of looking at themselves with 'friendly eyes'. For instance, pay attention to the way in which most players criticize their own game after the end of a match. They hardly pay attention to the things that went well at all.

Of course it is important to look critically, but that does not have to be linked to a negative feeling. It has been proven that by constantly stimulating your brain in a positive manner, you will influence and strengthen the neurons in your advantage. It's a peculiar way of thinking to call all the mistakes you make 'bad', when this will constantly stimulate your brain in a negative fashion. Good mistakes exist!

PILLAR 2: GOOD MISTAKES

The second pillar of the Mindset method that can help to shift you into action thinking and to produce a balanced mindset, besides 'friendly eyes', is seeing your play in terms of 'good mistakes'. As we have already said, any change is bound to be accompanied by mistakes at first. These mistakes are actually part of the process of change. Living without making any mistakes would be about as much fun as a tea-party in a graveyard. It seems clear to us that a willingness to learn from mistakes is far preferable to an attitude of leaving everything the same because it gives you a sense of security.

The concept of 'good mistakes' goes far beyond considering intentions more important than results (for instance when you hit a ball with the right intention but it lands just out). Many Olympic athletes interviewed in Beijing said that they were always looking for ways of learning from their mistakes. When asked what had gone wrong, their voices betrayed a striking lack of emotion. They analyzed objectively what had gone 'wrong' and explained how they expected to be able to learn from this to perform better in the future. They admitted that things had not gone as they had hoped. Still, they were not angry or annoyed with themselves, since they had done what lay within their power at that time. We use this concept to help players shift into action thinking. For instance, if you hit a deep ball to your opponent's weak backhand, and the ball lands just out, that is a 'good mistake'. This ball shows the right attitude, even though it was not yet perfectly executed. It is better than a short lob that lands well in, but that reflects fear and uncertainty.

Focusing on 'good mistakes' is investing in your game. That is not to deny that a more defensive approach may sometimes be more sensible. But if you constantly adjust your game because of tension and fall back on certainties, you will never make the progress you are hoping for.

Much the same applies at a higher level. A competitive player keeps losing baseline rallies after long duels. He can choose to react in one of three ways. Options 1 and 2 preserve a sense of hope and therefore sustain motivation. The player looks at himself with friendly eyes and good mistakes. In option 3 there is no hope, and so discouragement sets in – along with 'unfriendly eyes' and 'bad mistakes'.

1. He keeps to the same tactics; he hopes and believes that his fortunes will change, so that he can eventually start winning the points. He believes that he is fitter than the other player, or he may trust that the situation will improve once his game settles down and he gets into his own rhythm as the match progresses. This approach gives him hope, which will keep him motivated.

2. He decides to go to the net more often in the hope of being able to score, even though volleying is not his strongest point. This change in tactics gives him hope, increasing his motivation.

3. He gets fed up with the fact that he can't win from the baseline. He sees no way out of the situation, and has no ideas for improving or changing it. He gradually loses hope, and so discouragement sets in.

You can improve the mental aspect of your game enormously if you learn to watch your own game with 'friendly eyes' and apply the concept of 'good mistakes', without constantly reproaching yourself for the mistakes you make. Often, the truth is simply that your opponent is playing better, and instead of wallowing in self-chastisement, by retaining a spirit of curiosity, you could keep trying to find new opportunities. If you make good mistakes and watch yourself with 'friendly eyes', it will increase your self-respect. Besides enjoying yourself more in sport, you will find your self-confidence growing. As a result, you will also achieve more.

Playing field or battlefield?

Emotions during a match are frequently intense and confusing. That is partly because people are confronted with themselves and their limitations. And it is partly because when we start playing a match, we think we are doing something for fun, whereas the game frequently ends up more like a theatre of war. We hope to convince readers that it is possible to see the sports arena as a playing field rather than a battlefield. This will reduce tension and help you to gain more enjoyment as well as improving your game. You will be investing in yourself and your game, which will lead to progress in the long term. There is far more to be won than the match.

Winning simply by keeping the ball in play and waiting for your opponent to make mistakes may be a very strong tactical approach, but it can also be very unsatisfying and feel more like losing. Losing from a strong opponent while trying to play a well thought-out tactical game, giving everything and stretching yourself to the limit, may feel like winning. You can start to see winning and losing in a new light, and put them in perspective.

The following table contrasts aspects of story thinking and action thinking. It is intended to provide some initial guidelines. We are talking about shifts of emphasis here, not absolute opposites.

For instance, rationalizing still has a role to play in action thinking (though a more modest one), but visualizing is the dominant mode. In story thinking, the emphasis is on training purely to improve technique. In action thinking, the emphasis shifts to developing a balanced mind by applying the pillars and concentration forms. One side-effect of this shift is that it speeds up the development of better technique.

Story thinking	Action thinking
past/future	now / present
judgment	observation
rationalization	visualization
absent	alert/focus
noise	calm
verbalization	trigger-words
technique	self-knowledge
physical	mental
holding on	letting go
consumerism	investment
tense	relaxed
control	confidence
stubbornness	creativity
frustration	acceptance

Changing your mindset

Chapter 3 will be devoted entirely to the contrast between story thinking and action thinking. But first, in chapter 2, we shall explore the link between pillars 3 and 4 of the Mindset method, curiosity and self-knowledge. A realistic self-image, only to be achieved by being curious about yourself, is essential to making a good start on changing your mindset.

You can now practise friendly eyes and good mistakes by using the assignments on the following pages.

Pillar 1: Friendly eyes during sport

Make the effort, in every match and training session, to look at the way you're playing with friendly eyes. As soon as you notice that you are starting to beat yourself up and are becoming irritated with your game, look at your actions with friendly eyes. That means accepting that you can't do more than your best and that every action is part of a learning process. You know that this learning process will help you progress, which means that every action (successful or not) is part of your development. This acceptance alone induces a better match mentality. If you continually pay attention to this, you will notice a dramatic change in your attitude on the court or field. In the longer term, your game is bound to improve. Roger Federer has explained that it took him two years to find the 'right feeling' after he had decided (at the age of twenty-one) to deal differently with his emotions. He wanted to express his emotions, but not with 'judgmental eyes' or 'hostile eyes'. As a result, he initially ended up feeling rather 'flat'. We hope that these remarks will encourage you to persevere. Playing with friendly eyes is not something you can learn in a week, but you will notice a steady improvement over time. Believe in it.

Pillar 1: Friendly eyes in everyday life

Try this. For two whole weeks, look at your work or family situation with friendly eyes. Impress upon yourself that you are in principle doing your best and making a real effort, even though things always turn up that prevent you from doing exactly what you had planned, and seem to cause you to revert to old patterns of behaviour. People often tend to exaggerate the things that go wrong, which has the effect of paralysing them (just as on a court or field!). Try not to play down your successes and other good results; see them instead as the well-earned fruits of your efforts. Go up to someone you would normally treat coolly, and greet them enthusiastically. Observe the way this change affects this person. Don't pass judgment. Consider the following two attitudes; there's a big difference between them: 'All sorts of things came up, which prevented me from doing what I wanted to do.' 'In spite of all the things that came up, I did really well!'

Friendly eyes

Don't be like a prickly cactus!
Use friendly eyes for yourself and your opponent.

Pillar 2: good mistakes during sport

You may often find that you hold yourself in during a match, for fear of making mistakes. This creates problems as the pressure starts to rise. Try instead to be more daring. If you make a mistake because you allowed yourself to be a bit too rash, see it as a good mistake, because your intentions were good. These 'mistakes' are better than actions full of fear and tense control. Keep your motivation high, in spite of losing the point, by repeating constantly that it was a good mistake and that you're making progress. Eventually you will learn how to strike the right balance between being rash and timid.

Pillar 2: good mistakes in everyday life

Irritations may crop up at work or in your family, and you do nothing to change them; it's common enough. You just allow the situation to drag on in the hope that the problems will solve themselves. Unfortunately, they seldom do. Instead, take the initiative and try to communicate about these irritations. If you notice that your efforts are not appreciated, don't see it as failing, but as a good mistake. Keep daring to make these kind of good mistakes; don't give up. You tried to bring things up, with the best of intentions, and although it did not (yet) have the desired effect, you tried to change something unpleasant instead of just accepting the situation in passive resignation. In the end, your openness will bear fruit and make it easier to discuss things. In the long term, this will improve what you experienced as a difficult situation, even though it may not seem that way at first.

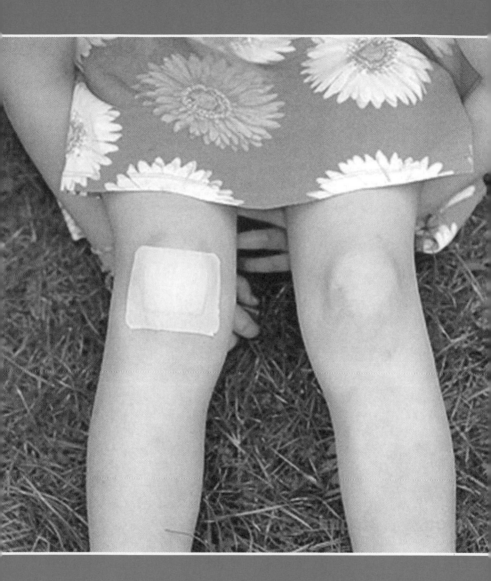

Good mistakes

When children make mistakes, it's ok.
Treat yourself in the same fashion.

MINDSET IN PRACTICE:
A MENTAL WARMING-UP

Mindset has a number of set procedures to ensure that you are in action thinking at the start of each training session or match. We call it a mental warming-up.

Before you walk into the sporting arena, prepare yourself mentally for exactly what you expect of yourself.

Example:
1. In a match, tactical or mental training session, decide to keep all your attention focused on the matter at hand, without analyzing technique.
2. When training technique, decide to focus all your attention on the change you're trying to achieve in your technique.

Whatever you're doing, always ensure that you look at yourself with friendly eyes and recognize good mistakes. Walk onto the court actively with the intention you've formulated beforehand clear in your mind.

Examples:
1. If you're chatting and looking all around you while walking onto the court, your mindset is not in action thinking.
2. If you walk onto the court with an active, vigorous step and clear goals, you will be in action thinking from the start of the training session or match.

Use silence as the background for your training session; this will help you achieve the best possible mindset.

Example:

Both you and your coach could try to use as few words as possible. Instead, communicate mainly through visual corrections (in other words, with the coach demonstrating a corrective movement without talking), and by deciding when and how to scan and zoom. This also means using trigger-words instead of long explanations. This will help you to base your training session on the concentration form feeling (bodily awareness) instead of thoughts.

Every time you walk into the sporting arena, you ask yourself two key questions:

1. What do I want to achieve today? Be specific about your goals.
2. What do I expect of my mindset/attitude during the training session?

CHAPTER 2

IT'S YOUR GAME

CURIOSITY IS A PREREQUISITE FOR SELF-KNOWLEDGE

In this chapter you learn that you can take charge of your own game, provided you gain insight into your real abilities.

'Only if you row to the other side of the sea will you find out who you really are', says Confucius. This is a rather tall order for most of us, but perhaps cycling to the sports field might be enough. While you are playing a match, you will not only discover a lot about yourself, but you will also start to realize that this self-knowledge (pillar 4) is a prerequisite for improving your game. However many lessons you take and training sessions you subject yourself to, if you don't try to acquire more self-knowledge, much of the effect will be lost. And you are the only person who can do that: it's your game! Perhaps we ought to turn Confucius's saying around: you can't row to the other side of the sea until you know who you really are. Because the only way to set realistic goals for yourself is to gain insight into your own abilities. Self-knowledge, attained by being curious (pillar 3), prevents you from overestimating or underestimating your own level of play. Self-knowledge is the beginning of a process in which frustration gradually gives way to acceptance and self-confidence. What will help you more than anything else to make constant progress in your game, and to enjoy doing so, is to develop a realistic self-image and to be interested in yourself. Some players have a much too negative self-image. They feel lacking in talent and believe there is little to be done about it. Others have an unrealistic picture of themselves and imagine that they could do things that are beyond the reach of Roger Federer. In both cases, the players leave the court feeling utterly demoralised.

The following sad anecdote illustrates people's tendency to leave things as they are, displaying little curiosity and shying away from change.

> A woman sits at the window waiting for her husband to come home. She knows that when he returns he will be drunk and beat her. One day she sees a woman pass by who is wearing a coat that looks just like hers, and she realizes with a shock that she might have been walking there herself. She goes to the hall cupboard, puts on her coat and opens the front door. When she opens the door, she recoils at all the possibilities that might present themselves in her new life. She closes the door, takes her coat off again, and takes up her old place at the window, once again waiting for her husband to come home.

Fear of the unknown or the unfamiliar can paralyze us and nip all kinds of growth in the bud. The certainty of old patterns – however destructive and frustrating they may be – seems preferable to creativity and courage and the curiosity that is needed to begin the change. How often do we not see this occur in everyday life, and in sport?

In the course of his sports career, a player keeps trying to acquire new skills. His initial reaction is often: 'it doesn't feel right'. But what feels right and what is right may not be the same thing. The fact that something feels 'strange' does not mean that there is something wrong with it. Remember the woman in the story.

To keep making this effort, curiosity is the first and most important condition. It may be hard to imagine, but one of the things you hear most often from sportsmen and sportswomen of all levels after a disappointing performance is: 'My game just wasn't working today!' Nothing else. With that attitude, you will never make any progress. Exactly what 'wasn't working'? Why not? Who might help me to make some change? What does my coach think? What can I do myself to change things for the better? Only someone who displays curiosity has a real chance of improving his or her game.

Curiosity about your own capabilities is the most important precondition for change. If you are not curious about why things keep repeating themselves, you will never be able to change them. If you think that things 'just happen to me', this arises from a lack of interest in yourself.

Consumerism or investment?

What do we mean by 'consumerism', and how does it have an adverse effect on sport? Players – from beginners to top professionals – often have inappropriate expectations of their coach. They shift all responsibility for their game to the coach, as if learning were like buying goods in a shop. The fact is you can't buy technique, but you can change your mindset, which will also improve your technique. Many players want to train technique a lot of the time and tactics some of the time, in the hope that their game will automatically improve.

It is often assumed that players can only bring about a change in their technique during a lesson. Many players believe that they can only make the necessary improvements with constant individual attention. Even if they are on the court four times a week outside the lessons, it is only under the coach's supervision that they pay proper attention to improving technique. When playing 'for fun' or practising with a regular partner, they play without setting any goals at all. This is what we call consumerism. A player who invests in his game should constantly be practising improvements in technique, not only in lesson time.

What is wrong with simply training technique? Nothing. But some players regard this kind of training as the only key to success, and that is what holds them back. You should not believe that merely turning up for a training session is enough to ensure progress. Training will certainly improve your ball sense, but if you pay no attention to the mental aspects of the game, your progress will be minimal. Many players of all standards think along these lines: 'I have an important tournament next week. My backhand and my service are not working so well. I'll take two lessons and everything will be fine.' This approach is doomed to failure.

Example of club player (consumerism)

Coach: 'What do you want to work on for the next half-hour?' (Thinks: *He has paid a lot of money for this private lesson so I must provide the service he wants*').

Player: 'Well, there are several aspects of my game I'm unhappy about' (Thinks: *I paid a lot of money for this lesson, so I've got to get as much as possible out of it*').

Coach: 'So what do you want to work on in particular?'

Player: 'Well my backhand is completely useless, we really need to look at that. And I want to be able to hit a great topspin forehand. Apart from that, my first serve goes out too often and my second serve is too weak.'

Coach: 'Right!'

Player: 'And my volleys are just not good enough. I keep missing them. And perhaps we ought to do a few smashes.'

Coach: 'Hmm, we'd better get started then, before the half-hour is over!'

Example of a professional player (consumerism)

Rising star leaves the court after losing a match.

Star: 'Well thank you very much. You said I needed to make a minor technical adjustment to my second serve to make it a bit safer, and instead, I end up hitting a double fault on a big point. Brilliant periodization. It would have made much more sense to introduce the change after this tournament.'

Coach: 'You know you have to invest in your game. You want to get into the top fifty, don't you?'

Star: 'Yeah sure, but not with you. You're fired!'

The pillars: do you apply them as a consumer or as an investor?

How should the pillars be applied? Do you practise self-deception by always seeing yourself in the best possible light, or do you look honestly at how things are, instead of at how you want them to be? Experience with many Mindset training sessions over the years has taught us that players unconsciously put their heads in the sand when they want to change their behaviour in some fundamental way. It's important to be on your guard for this ostrich-type behaviour. Players tend to lapse into the consumer's role, and into story thinking when facing hard challenges about their behaviour patterns. The following paragraphs look at these two roles, consumer versus investor, and try to explain them in more detail.

People who adopt the consumer's role look for the cause of their behaviour anywhere but in themselves. While they want to change their game (i.e. their behaviour), they adopt a passive attitude and expect solutions to come from outside (e.g. from the coach). Someone who adopts the role of investor, on the other hand, looks within himself for causes ('It's your game!'). Consuming and investing are complete opposites.

Consuming / Story thinking	Investing / Action thinking
judgmental / hostile eyes	friendly eyes
lazy mistakes	good mistakes
indifference	curiosity
ignorance	self-knowledge
boredom	self-discipline
complacency (=passive)	acceptance (=active)

'Consumer' types, with their 'judgmental/hostile' eyes, indulge themselves and blame disappointing results on external factors (the coach, the opponent, the umpire/referee, team-mates, the wind, et cetera). They are also very quick to express their opinion about everything around them; they never stop 'judging'. Investors, on the other hand, observe objectively without passing judgment.

We can clearly see the difference between these two attitudes by looking at 'lazy mistakes'. Consumers are lazy and see all their mistakes as 'good mistakes'; after all, they were simply doing their best. They don't take responsibility for their actions. Investors analyze their intentions. If the intention was good, but the way it was carried out was not perfect, it was a good mistake. But if the intention was not good (lazy/timid/cowardly), it was not a good mistakes. The investor will look at this honestly and seek the solution within himself, without using hostile eyes.

'Indifference' is a typical consumer-type response. It comes out in answers like 'no idea', 'I don't know' and 'yes, but'. Looking at yourself honestly and critically is alien to consumers. Displaying real curiosity by asking open questions (how does that happen, do you think, what do you think I should do?) is a sign of an investor.

Consumers do not possess 'self-knowledge', since they have no 'curiosity'. Consumers are therefore 'ignorant'.

Consumers do have 'self-discipline', but only because it adds a protective layer they need to carry on displaying consumer-type behaviour. It is the self-discipline of the man or woman who spends a fortune on diet pills without thinking of the cause of his or her excess kilos. Self-discipline is considered boring.

A world famous investor is the actress Julie Andrews. She says: 'Some people regard discipline as a chore. For me, it is a kind of order that sets me free to fly'.

For investors, 'acceptance' is an active step. In the case of a consumer, acceptance means complacency (passive, with little self-criticism).

This entire book is about *investment*, and it will give many real-life examples of this mindset. The following table provides some real-life examples of *consumers'* behaviour.

Judgmental or hostile eyes as opposed to friendly eyes.	Someone who believes that he is constantly looking at himself with friendly eyes describes his match as follows: 'I was playing way over my level, and realized I would never be able to keep it up'. This player was unconsciously condemning himself to playing at his 'normal' level. So looking with judgmental eyes can also mean not allowing yourself to play really well. Another comment often heard after a match is 'the opponent was really annoying (such a cheat, so arrogant et cetera).' When a player looks at his opponent with hostile eyes, this will effect his own balance of mind(set) and therefore be derogatory to his game and concentration.
Lazy mistakes as opposed to good mistakes	When a pupil was asked why he didn't position himself well for the ball on an important point, which resulted in an unforced error, he reacts as follows. 'No idea, it was a really difficult ball, you can't expect me to be in a great position every single time.' The truth is often different: the player didn't make the mental and physical effort needed to execute the shot. A lazy mistake.

Indifference as opposed to curiosity	A player was asked what she thought happened when she lost the match after leading 6-4, 6-2. She replied, 'No idea. I really don't know. It just happened.' This hardly reflects an attitude of curiosity.
Ignorance as opposed to self-knowledge	'I just don't get it. I threw everything at it. New racket, trained for hours, et cetera. To have lost this match is just unacceptable.' This player displays a lack of self-knowledge, since there is little curiosity as to the 'deeper' reasons for the loss.
Boredom as opposed to self-discipline	'I've been training these tactics for weeks now; it's so one-sided.'
Complacency as opposed to acceptance	'The balls are just not working for me today. Oh well, nothing much to do about it. I don't feel like carrying on.' The underlying idea seems to be: 'You can't make yourself feel like it, can you?' But suppose a surgeon didn't 'feel like' performing an operation? Acceptance is quite different from complacency.

PILLAR 4: SELF-KNOWLEDGE

The contents of your suitcase

You go to the court to play a match. Compare it to going on holiday. All you have is in your suitcase, nothing else. If you didn't have a winning service before you left, you won't have one when you arrive at your destination.

Let's look at two examples of ways in which a club player may deal with the contents of his 'suitcase'. Don't forget that sport consists of four factors: **mentality, tactics, fitness and technique**. Of course, we are not suggesting that it isn't a good idea to improve your serving technique (or any other stroke); all we're saying is that the 'consumer' often has to invest more in mental factors than he realizes or is willing to do.

> The mindset of this recreational player clearly belongs to story thinking
>
> A player keeps hitting his first serve as hard as possible, and only twenty percent of them are going in. His second serve is far too soft, so he almost always loses the point. He decides to change his approach. He is going to do something that is not in his suitcase, which is to hit his second serve harder. He carries on losing just as many points as before, but now from double faults. After the match he decides to take two lessons to learn how to hit a second

serve with topspin. When he applies his new second serve in the next match, he discovers it's still not in his suitcase. He still keeps on hitting double faults. What would this player do, if he were to apply the action thinking? After the match, the player decides to discuss his experience with a coach who understands the mental side of tennis. This coach suggests dealing realistically with what he already has in his suitcase. It would be better to hit his first serve a little less hard, to increase the percentage of balls that go in. If eighty percent of his first serves go in, even if they are not hit at full strength, this will immediately boost the player's self-confidence, which will generally have the added effect of improving the second serve.

In the long term it will pay dividends to change your technique, but this is a long process that requires patience and perseverance. The point we are making here is simply that what feels right and what is right are two different things at that moment in time. Obviously the player would much rather hit his service at full strength. But you need to have a certain acceptance during a match. A long period of investment after the match will be needed to boost development further.

Showing respect for your opponent and acquiring self-knowledge

The determination to win a match at any price may blind a player and distort his assessment of his own strength and that of his opponent. Understanding yourself in every aspect of your game also means being able to assess your own strength in relation to your opponent. If you lose a match, your opponent was the better player at that point, that is all there is to it. Often players who have lost a match frequently show too little respect for their opponent. By constantly making excuses or belittling your opponent you will ultimately undermine your self-respect.

Example of a club player (someone who lacks a realistic image of his own strength and has no respect for his opponent)
'We ought to call Alex Mr Moonball! Those high, loopy balls to the back of the court all through the match, it drives me crazy. And I'm not the only one. Everyone hates playing him. None of my strokes worked, but how could they? You can't call that tennis! I don't mind losing from a better player,

but losing from someone who plays much worse than I do, that's really frustrating.'

Example of a competitive or professional player (someone who lacks a realistic image of his own strength and has no respect for his opponent)

'It's always the same boring routine with those Spanish players. All they do is hit topspin, topspin and more topspin. From every corner and in every situation. You just can't get a real game going. I don't understand that they can't play more creatively, like I do. I will never be such a one-sided, boring player.'

Stages of learning

Let's look at the process of gaining more insight into your own capabilities. The following table is often used for the different phases of learning.

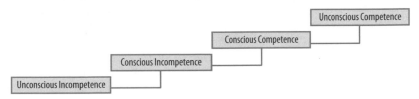

A player who has a good grasp of this process will approach his development in a far more conscious way. He will constantly have to go back to the table and keep applying it to each part of his game to reach a higher level. In general, this is the meaning of the different stages:

Unconscious Incompetence (UI): you don't know you can't do something. You are unaware of not having the skill.

Conscious Incompetence (CI): you know you can't do something. You are aware that you do not posess the skill yet.

Conscious Competence (CC): you can do something if you really concentrate. If you are consciously aware you are mostly capable of mastering the skill.

Unconscious Competence (UC): you can do something well without having to think about it (reflex). You are instinctively master of the skill.

The following examples are based on a match situation. We could easily come up with dozens of other examples, at any level of play, but this example will quickly clarify what the terms in the table mean in a practical situation. The examples illustrate mentality, tactics, fitness, and technique, in that order. 'Unconscious incompetence' can be quite funny!

	Unconscious Incompetence	Conscious Incompetence	Conscious Competence	Unconscious Competence
Mentality	Mentality, what's that got to do with tennis?	I always seem to have a negative attitude on the court.	If I find myself getting negative, I can usually catch myself in time and turn it around into a positive attitude.	People say that I always seem positive and dynamic on the court.
Tactics	I enjoy hitting the ball back and forth in a match. Feels great when I hit it right on the sweet spot. Funny that I never seem to win.	I keep hitting the ball to my opponent's strong side, but I don't seem able to stop doing so.	If I concentrate, I regularly succeed in playing the ball to my opponent's weak spot.	My opponent doesn't like playing against me, because apparently I'm always able to find his weak side.
Fitness	Tennis is really not a strenuous sport. It never makes me tired.	I get so tired playing tennis that I hardly ever win a third set.	If I go running once a week and do my interval training, I still feel fit in the third set.	My opponents often say that they hate the idea of playing a third set against me.
Technique	I can't figure out why my technique's still rubbish; I've had at least twenty lessons.	My grip's not right, so there's no topspin on my backhand.	If I consciously change my grip to the backhand grip, I can usually manage to hit my backhand with topspin.	I can use my topspin backhand whenever I want.

Here is an anecdote that everyone will recognize. Try to decide which of the above boxes it belongs in. Is the player at the stage of conscious competence, conscious incompetence or unconscious incompetence, and in which elements of the game (mentality, tactics, fitness, technique)?

> **Club player**
> 'What a pathetic performance, the way Frank plays. I'll show him what real tennis is. One more of those measly little balls and I'll smash him off the court. I'll have his eyes popping out of his head, he won't know where he is. Come on then, with that useless second serve. Jesus, what a moonball! This is going to be a real killer. Boing! That was terrific! Oh, I overdid it a bit. I wacked it in the fence.'

The answer is that this player is at the stage of unconscious incompetence in all areas: mentality, tactics, fitness and technique.

What are the causes underlying this player's unconscious incompetence? Let's look at each area in turn. UI= Unconscious Incompetence.

UI mentality: overestimates his own abilities; is busy judging his opponent instead of concentrating on the ball.

UI tactics: chooses the wrong stroke; flat instead of using topspin; wants to score straight away (although there is no opening for doing so) instead of putting his opponent under pressure first.

UI fitness: arm moves too slowly to generate enough speed off the racket-face (shoulder and arm muscles not sufficiently well-trained) to give the ball enough topspin; abdominal muscles too slack (i.e. not sufficiently well-trained) to stay in balance while hitting the ball.

UI technique: racket face too open at the point of impact; the body doesn't stay low long enough while hitting the ball.

If you recognize problems in your game, in any area, you have already taken the first, important step in the right direction, since you have gone from unconscious incompetence to conscious incompetence. Sometimes this does not feel particularly good at the time, but that will change, you are opening doors to improvement.

Our method aims at consciousness-raising, with the ultimate aim of playing unconsciously. 'Unconscious competence' in sport means playing instinctively.

To actually set change in motion and to accomplish it calls for creativity and courage. For the time being, it is sufficient to know that it means breaking with old habits. Players may say, for instance: 'I simply have an aggressive game.' But sometimes patience is required before you can go on the attack. Being capable of patience does not mean that you're not an aggressive player, it means that you possess creativity and insight. A player who lacks this flexibility will find it hard to make the transition from being consciously incompetent to consciously competent and unconsciously competent.

Pillar 3: Curiosity during sport

When you're talking to your coach, do you sometimes find yourself answering with 'yes, but'? 'Yes, but' is the opposite of curiosity. If you notice yourself doing this, stop yourself and try saying instead: 'Yes, and how do you think things might be different?' The same applies to responses like 'I don't know'. This reflects little openness and self-knowledge. Instead of saying 'I don't know', try to form your own opinion. Even if it is wrong, at least make the effort to think of a solution and display interest and passion. That will always have a positive effect on your interaction.

Pillar 3: Curiosity in everyday life

Try to listen to the person you're talking to. This may sound obvious, but if you pay attention, you'll notice you spend more time interpreting than actually listening. You fill everything in, because you have a picture of the person. Make a determined decision to really listen, not to interrupt, not to fill in the gaps yourself. What is the person actually saying? Ask more questions or just be silent, if something is not entirely clear. You can ask open questions like 'what do you mean?' or 'what would you do if...?' You'll soon notice that you are rewarded with other people's surprising and original ideas, which you would otherwise have missed.

Curiosity

It might be a little bit scary to take a closer look, but it's also exhilarating!

Pillar 4: Self-knowledge during sport and in everyday life

Grade yourself from 1 – 5 (1=low, 5=high) in the following chart. Fill it in twice: once as an athlete, and once as a private person. It is possible to score high (or low) in the opposites, for example you can score high in friendly eyes and also high in judgmental eyes.

This assignment is meant to heighten your awareness. Let your coach and your partner also fill in the chart for you.

Story thinking	1	2	3	4	5	Action thinking	1	2	3	4	5
judgmental eyes						friendly eyes					
lazy mistakes						good mistakes					
indifference						curiosity					
ignorance						self-knowledge					
boredom						self-discipline					
complacency						acceptance					
negative						positive					
insecure						self-confident					
giving up						persevering					
impatient						patient					
full of doubt						with conviction					
apathetic						motivated					
stubborn						flexible					
fearful						courageous					
predictable						creative					
dependent						autonomous					
easily distracted						focused					

6 Pillars

Self-knowledge

Is the truth always what you see in the mirror?
Ask your coach, partner or friends.

CHOOSING A GOOD COACH

To make progress, it is essential to find a good coach. People often pay too little attention to this. It is better to have a good coach even for only one session a month than to have a bad coach three times a week – provided that you have the discipline to do what has been agreed upon during practice sessions.

What do we mean by a good coach? Someone who:
1. is enthusiastic and motivates you (using friendly eyes and good mistakes); who gives compliments when appropriate.
   N.B. As soon as you notice that a coach keeps reacting negatively, you must bring it up. If he does not change his attitude, change to a different coach.
2. is curious, raises issues that need to be discussed, is not put off by criticism and dares to adopt a vulnerable position; understands interdependance.
3. can listen well and asks open questions, which can help you come up with solutions yourself;
4. dares to take the lead, confronts you when necessary, takes difficult decisions and does not keep putting things off.
5. is actively involved in developing himself as a coach, and who will consult a colleague if necessary or bring in a fitness trainer, sports psychologist, dietician et cetera.
6. regularly asks you for feedback about his or her advice;
7. is involved in your game and your progress in all areas;
8. is always on time and never cancels without giving a good, explicit reason;
9. is willing to exchange views about short-term and long-term goals;

10. can give you simple, goal-oriented 'homework' in the form of assignments and ways of practising, so that you can carry on your training independently;
11. who does not give you too much information at once; who knows when to leave out things that are not relevant.
12. who maps out a clear course together with you, for the short and longer term;
13. who is a fully qualified coach;
14. who regularly comes to watch your matches or who creates match situations in the training sessions.
15. who never has his mobile phone on during lessons (except of course under exceptional circumstances).

What are your own responsibilities in relation to the coach?
1. To communicate well and clearly, to help forge a relationship of trust;
2. To keep to what has been agreed, when it comes to practice material and training outside the lessons;
3. Always to arrive well in time for your lesson. This means that all your material is ready before you go on to the court, and that your mindset is focused on what you want to learn;
4. For you, as a player, it is essential to receive good advice. This often happens outside the lessons. It is important to realize that this is professional help and should be paid accordingly. Coaches often lack the business sense to make this clear, so that discussions of this kind do not take place. But this is a pity, since it detracts from your progress;
5. To give positive feedback when something is working and to make it clear when it is not;
6. To be totally dedicated during your lessons, your training sessions and matches; using a mental warming up as described in intermezzo 1.
7. To make sure that all business matters are arranged clearly and properly.
8. If you plan to change to another coach or to stop altogether, start by notifying your present coach first, explain the reasons for your decision, and thank him or her for the work he or she has put in.

If you read through the above points and agree with them, write down answers to the following questions:

1. Why have I chosen my present coach?
2. Can I achieve progress in the mental side of my game with him/her?
3. What is his/her added value for me?
4. Do I behave in the correct manner to my coach? If not, what is wrong with my attitude and am I willing to change this? Reflect on what changes you would like to bring about.

CHAPTER 3

PLAYING TENNIS WITH A BEARD

THE BALLAST OF THINKING TOO MUCH

This chapter provides insight into the origins of your fear and insecurities and teaches how you can start to overcome them

Many people start it as soon as they wake up and are still going strong when they lie down to go to sleep: they are editing a film in their heads. The film is made up of thoughts and emotions related to their past and future. It is rattling on incessantly, even on the sports field. That is what we call story thinking, and the metaphor we use for it is the malfunctioning machine. Once we have achieved mindfulness, this mode of thought no longer applies; its place has been taken by action thinking. Action thinking focuses on the 'now'. The player has managed to banish all distracting thoughts and is fully immersed in the moment. This is not something that can be done at the drop of a hat. It requires years of concentrated effort, a process of trial and plenty of mistakes. This book essentially provides a mental plan, a series of stages towards attaining the 'now'. The result is what happens to a tennis player in top form who hits an ace – exactly as he had seen it in his mind before he actually hit his service. This is called visualization. If you have never had this experience with an ace, you are sure to recognize it with some other stroke. The point is that you feel instinctively beforehand what is going to happen, and it does.

Many readers will remember the legendary goal that Marco van Basten scored against the Soviet Union in the final of the 1988 European Soccer Championship. It was one of the finest goals of all time. In a TV documentary, Van Basten explains that his strike was no coincidence.

His shot at goal was carefully 'aimed and timed'. Closer analysis reveals that the ball soared about ten centimetres above the hands of Dasayev, the best keeper in the tournament, and dipped five centimetres below the crossbar. An almost impossible achievement. Van Basten explained that when Mühren passed the ball to him, the insight came to him (in… sight = visualization) that it was possible.

PLAYING TENNIS WITH A BEARD

In his essay collection *Het sadistische universum* ('The sadistic universe', 1964), the Dutch novelist W.F. Hermans recalls an anecdote about a man with a remarkably fine beard from Alphonse Allais's story 'La barbe'. One day, a girl asks this proud owner of one of the most magnificent beards in Paris whether he sleeps with his beard inside his blanket or on top of it. The poor man has never given the matter a moment's thought. That night, when he goes to bed, he can't sleep. He lays his beard on top of the blanket, then puts it underneath, but he just can't fall asleep. He parts his beard in two, placing some above and some below the blankets, but in vain. However much he manoeuvres his beard, his confusion and compulsive thoughts keep getting worse and worse, and he is totally incapable of sleep.

Hermans goes on to comment that one can easily guess how the man finally ends his torment, after a long series of sleepless nights. The only solution remaining to him is a visit to the barber's. The radical removal of his beard will finally solve his insomnia.

The radical removal of story thinking is the only way in which we can solve our problem of tensing up, 'choking' and over-consciousness. Unfortunately, most active participants in sport, at all levels, think too much. This is a form of ballast which undermines our enjoyment and our game.

To let this really sink in, let's take another look at the table printed in chapter 1. Many of the contrasts will now have become far clearer.

Story thinking	Action thinking
past / future	now / present
judgment	observation
rationalization	visualization
absent	alert/focus
noise	calm
verbalization	trigger-words
technique	self-knowledge
physical	mental
holding on	letting go
consumerism	investment
tense	relaxed
control	confidence
stubbornness	creativity
frustration	acceptance
ego	being

The last contrast on the list needs a little explanation. The ego is a breeding-ground for stories, and the ego lives on stories. It constantly feeds and defines itself by story thinking. Without this thinking it would evaporate, and the ego is so constructed that it will do anything to avoid this fate. That is why it is so hard to reach the story-less 'now' – to achieve just 'being', as Buddhists say. Everyone knows the phenomenon of 'grumbling at yourself': this is the ego blatantly at work. Ego and story thinking are two sides of the same coin. But it is not a winning coin, since they lead only to frustration, loss of concentration, and as a result to poorer play. The ego verbalizes, rationalizes and judges. It is fondest of mechanisms that strengthen it, like commenting, criticizing and complaining. These magnify the ego, but they also magnify your sense of frustration. The ego benefits from frustration and anger. There are tried and tested ways of silencing the ego and its story thinking: concentrate on your breathing, visualization, positive reinforcement ('trigger-words') and developing rituals.

Thinking with your body

Let's go back to the player who hits an ace. He has seen precisely before-hand (visualization) where he wants to play the ball. It just happens. This is sometimes called 'flow': it happens when the mind is free of thought and has changed into pure, non-judgmental observation. Inner noise has been replaced by a sense of calm. Mind (thought) and body (action) come together. The state of flow is that of continuous direct observation, without judgment or bias. You could also call it 'total presence' or 'total alertness'. It expresses itself in a perfect sense of ease in the sporting arena. Players often experience flow during training sessions. That is because there is no emotional attachment to points, as in a match. It is a playing-field situation, not a battlefield. You might say that in this state, sport is a dynamic form of meditation: it is played in the 'now' without judgments or fears intervening to muddy the experience.

Why do athletes often enjoy training sessions more than matches?

Perhaps it has now become clear why training is often so much more fun than playing matches, and why you often play so much better in them. In matches, past and future may play a prominent role (story think-ing). Training sessions generally take place in the now (action thinking). Action thinking is thinking with your body; the aim is to deactivate the process of rational thinking, leaving the action to the body, the subcon-scious. This means, for instance, deploying technique unconsciously rather than consciously. We need to develop a child's relationship to our body, learning playfully and applying what we have learned.

This only applies, of course, when you are 'grooving' your strokes, not when you are changing your technique. If you are working on getting more depth and rhythm into your strokes, you can allow your body to do its work completely 'unconsciously'. But if you want to change your grip, you have to start by doing so consciously. The aim should be to make the switch from conscious to unconscious as fast as possible. Once you are working with action thinking, your body has an opportunity to perform its move-ments in a smooth and relaxed way. If you are 'over-conscious' of changing your grip, you are in story thinking, and the movement will feel wooden.

Making the mental switch from story to action thinking will fundamentally transform your experience and your level of play in a match. It will also affect your progress in training sessions.

What are the specific consequences of this change of mindset on the sporting arena?

What many players do not realize is that performing is linked to an extremely complex mental state. 'Oh really, that's just a question of technique!' people will often say. 'Performing badly just means you need more practice to improve your technique.' No, the technical execution of a stroke is influenced by the player's mental state. What may happen, for instance, in the brain of a player who is preparing to hit a backhand? He focuses on a technical aspect of the stroke: grip, swing, position, rotation of the body et cetera. This is a useful approach when training elements of technique, but in a match it may easily ruin your game. There is a considerable risk that this 'over-consciousness' may adversely affect the stroke during a match. This is story thinking. The player can prevent it by visualizing the path the ball will follow and the exact spot where it will hit the ground. Depending on his level, he visualizes the stroke and banishes all aspects of technique (which training sessions have put 'in his system' – the 'suitcase' in chapter 2) from his mental preparation for the stroke. This will greatly increase the likelihood of his producing a successful backhand. This is action thinking. And if the player misses the ball after all, he finds it far easier to accept, which means he has a far better chance of hitting the ball well the next time he encounters exactly the same situation. In this case, he will experience it as a 'good mistake'.

THE 5TH PILLAR: SELF-DISCIPLINE

To change your mindset, you need both self-discipline and courage. Everyone who reads the following paragraphs will see that the arguments they contain are plain common sense. The only way of making a concrete change to your mindset is with a healthy dose of self-discipline and a mental plan (see Chapter 9).

'I don't dare': what does that mean?

Players often say that having had a particular stroke or action in mind, they found that they 'didn't dare' to actually execute it. However convinced they may have been that a particular stroke or action was the right one, they lacked the courage to follow through. That is because they were already preparing a negative outcome in their minds – 'suppose I miss'. Since they are not in the here and now of action thinking, but in the future of story thinking: because they are not visualizing but rationalizing, they tense up and are no longer capable of completing the action that was intended. The malfunctioning machine takes over from the state of mindfulness. With heightened self-discipline the player can demand the right choice at the right moment. You can decide to be daring. Also if the player is prepared to release attachment to points it will help him achieve his best standard at every given moment.

Attachment to points

'I was 5-2 up, and had set point on my own serve. And then I went and served a double fault! I ended up losing the set and the match. I couldn't believe it. Here we go again. If I hadn't hit that one double fault, I would have won the match.'

How often do you not hear stories like that? Countless players have lost matches by tensing up as a result of being fixated on the score. It's a good idea to bear in mind that you should always play for the next point, and never for the game, the set or the match. Of course, the score may well influence your tactics; if you are well ahead, you can afford to take a bigger risk. But this is quite separate from becoming fixated on the score. That is what we mean here by 'attachment': the score becomes a 'story' that dominates the game.

Forget the score and concentrate on the only rally that matters: the one you're playing now. Whenever you find yourself thinking of the score during the match, try to put those thoughts aside. The instruments described in chapter 6 will help you make this step. As soon as you start focusing on the score, you lapse into story thinking, which will undermine your concentration.

What often happens if you have a strong attachment to someone? You start worrying that something may happen to him or her. All sorts of horror scenarios loom up if the person does not turn up on time. This is story thinking in its full-blown form. Everyone knows the negative influence of these pointless thoughts. Although it may seem far-fetched to compare this to an attachment to the score in a match, in fact exactly the same mechanism is at work here. This attachment gives rise to stories that undermine your concentration and mental balance. 'If only I hadn't…', 'Now I must really take care not to…', 'I wish I had never…'; everyone has had thoughts like this during a match. They cause you to tense up. You can scarcely lift your arm to serve. You want to put a ball away convincingly, but can't accelerate your arm movement. You want to get to a ball but find yourself rooted to the spot. Being attached to the score can paralyze you, and can cause you to 'choke'. You must learn to let go.

Letting go

'Letting go' is not denial but acceptance. You should not invest mental energy in things that you cannot influence. Don't become irritated about things that are unavoidable but accept them. The first step is to become conscious of the irritation. Try to see that irritation as a feeling that crops up, but don't identify with it. In other words, it is not part of your personality, your ego. It is simply something that comes your way, so that you can decide what to do with it. You are not identified with the irritation and so you can look at it from a distance. It is pointless to worry about what others think of you, about whether you are coming up to your own expectations, or about things that you have no power to change.

If you can't influence something, you need to learn to let it go. Don't blame things you can't influence, or which are just as annoying for your opponent as for yourself. If you do, you will only disrupt your balance and generate 'noise' in your head – story thinking – and your performance will suffer as a result.

Even professional players sometimes forget to let go

Here is a recent example of a professional player who had trouble letting go of something over which she had no influence.

In Wimbledon 2008, Jelena Jankovic's quarter-final match was assigned to court 18. She explained that this had preyed on her mind during the match. After suffering a heavy defeat, she commented: 'I don't know what they are doing, to put Venus on number 2 and I'm on number 18. I was almost playing in the parking lot. I almost needed a helicopter to get to my court.'

Things that you can't influence

- the weather;
- noises and other distractions outside the court;
- your opponent's behaviour: how he counts (or fails to count), where he stands to receive your serve, how little (or how much) time he takes to start playing each point, or the height at which he hits the balls (this is something over which you do have a little influence…);
- the spectators' behaviour: whether they are talking loudly or moving too much, that they only applaud for your opponent;
- the surface of the court or the court that the referee decided you would play on;
- the quality of the balls (in a tournament situation).

Things that you can influence

- your own material, ensuring it is well prepared beforehand, balls (only in practice sessions);
- ensuring that you have something to eat and drink with you;
- your game plan / tactics;
- your recovery time (in the changeover and in between points);
- your breathing / heartbeat;
- your preparation for the match: training, enough sleep, diet
- the degree to which you exert yourself;
- counting the score out loud;
- your emotions.

Once it becomes clear in your mind what you can let go of, everything becomes rather easier to handle. It is quite incredible how many things people can get wound up about. If you dare to let things go, you will be able to get the best out of yourself, whatever sport you play.

'Why am I simply incapable, again and again, of mustering the necessary discipline? I always seem to revert to the same old patterns as before.'

By becoming conscious of the benefits it will give you, on and off the sports field, you will acquire the energy needed to carry on. This investment will produce a concrete shift from story thinking to action thinking. Learn to enjoy the process of change.

Pillar 5: Self-discipline during sport

Over the next four weeks, maintain a constant awareness of your breathing during training sessions and matches; pay attention to how it changes when you're under pressure, and after a particular point. For instance: after a really tough point, take the time to slow your breathing down before starting on a new one. For clear instructions on this subject, see the section on 'breathing and pranayama' in chapter 6, where we discuss exactly how best to deal with your breathing. If you can muster the discipline to raise your awareness of your breathing for four weeks, we can guarantee that you will recover from each point more rapidly and be ready to start the next one.

Pillar 5: Self-discipline in everyday life

Make sure that all the right conditions are in place before starting a match. That may sound easy and obvious, but our experience, with professional players as well as people who play recreationally, often shows the opposite. We invite you to try out the following plan for four weeks. Make sure that you have taken care of everything that needs to be in order before a match. Anyone who takes part in a sport knows exactly what he or she has to do, but all too often, people leave things to the last minute. This causes a sense of agitation at the start of a match. If you improve your discipline in this area, it will help you to achieve a greater sense of inner calm. This assignment may sound rather simple, but we know from experience that it is often neglected and will help to get you off to a good start.

Discipline

Imagine if you leave out a couple of bricks...

IS THIS CHEATING? AND HOW TO DEAL WITH BAD CALLS?

Is it cheating when a player uses provocation, intentionally or unintentionally, to coax his opponent into story thinking? And what is the best way to deal with bad calls (real or assumed)?

During a Grade A tournament in Apeldoorn, Marina has flown through the first five games without a hitch. The score is 5-0 and everything is going brilliantly. She is winning her service games effortlessly, and will be serving for the set. She feels fine at the changeover, since all the precision-training on placing her serve has paid off. When she gets up from her stool and passes her opponent, the latter grins insincerely and says, 'I had no idea how good your service had become! It was nowhere near this good last time.' When Marina stands at the baseline, ready to serve, these words keep going through her head. 'I'll show her how good my service is', she thinks. And immediately starts the game with a double fault.

Marina was in action thinking and her opponent's remark caused her to lapse into story thinking. It's possible that her opponent had been deliberately trying to unsettle Marina, to make her feel uncertain and to disrupt her rhythm. How should we classify a deliberate attempt by a player to entice his opponent into story thinking? Is it a kind of cheating? Or is it a very clever way of disturbing your opponent's balance and turning the match around to your advantage? This device is used among club, intermediate and professional players, sometimes (but not always) intentionally, to disrupt the opponent's game.

The most spectacular example of the way in which even world-class soccer players may lapse into story thinking is the demise of Zinédine Zidane in the 2006 World Cup final between France and Italy. During extra time, with the score standing at 1-1, Zidane said contemptuously to the Italian defender Marco Materazzi, who kept pulling at his shirt, 'If you want my shirt so badly, you can have it after the match'. To which Materazzi replied, 'I'd rather have your sister'. This led to Zidane's notorious head butt, after which he was sent off the field. What exactly happened here? Both players lapsed into story thinking, and Zidane came off worst.

In most cases the provocation is subtler and the consequences are less direct, although they may frequently be dramatic. Let's look at some examples of ways in which we may encounter this behaviour in sport.

Exaggerated or insincere compliments can disturb your opponent's concentration and coax him into story thinking. Slyly shouting: 'Brilliant shot!' after a perfectly executed winning point by your opponent might tempt him to try the same thing again; but now he is too conscious of it and will attempt it as a story thinker. Another common tactic is creating the impression that you're not doing your best, or saying during the changeover how badly you're doing and that you normally play much better. This too may lead your opponent to lapse into story thinking. At the club level, a remark that could be annoying as it is off-putting, to a player who can't deal with the way you are slowing down the pace of the game, is: 'I'm never signing up for this low level again. I can't get into my game at all.' Another player might say, after his younger opponent has convincingly won the first game: 'This always happens to me against young players; they win the first game through overconfidence. Then they totally collapse.'

All these comments are intended to put the opponent off his game. The antidote is the same as our advice for shifting from story thinking into action thinking: try to get yourself into the here and now and to stay there, by using feeling (movement, trigger-words, rituals and visualization). You should be aware that the comments cannot affect you if you know what you should be focusing on. They're just empty words. Chapters 5 and 6 contain precise explanations for ways of preserving your concentration through 'feeling' in situations like this.

Bear in mind – recalling the example of Zidane – that these verbal tactics also have repercussions for the person using them. The person who has first started on this tack also runs the risk of lapsing into story thinking and not being able to play at his best. There is no one answer to the question of whether these verbal tactics should be classified as cheating or whether they belong to a player's normal arsenal of weapons. Each player determines how he wants to behave on court. If you would rather go through life with a reputation for good sportsmanship, you won't choose this approach. If you feel that the ends always justify the means of winning a match, you might do so. A mindset player would never choose this path, since situations of this kind do not even arise when you are in action thinking.

Dealing with bad calls (real or assumed): confrontation or clarity?

At all levels, players regularly make mistakes when calling balls in or out. That does not mean that they are cheating. Eagerness and emotion can lead you to literally 'see' the ball out. You don't look at the bounce, you know instinctively that the ball is going out (but unfortunately, emotions can deceive you!) and you call 'out!'. Bad calls of this kind are more frequent than players realize. We suspect that real cheating occurs less often than is generally believed. Former professional players as well as club and intermediate players were questioned about this subject, and almost all of them said that in their entire tennis career they had only encountered at most three players who really cheated, and some had met none at all. Still, many players have difficulty with their opponent's bad calls or with intimidating behaviour. We believe you can learn how to deal with this. In the first place, you have to really take on board the fact that your opponent has probably just made a mistake. This will immediately give you a different feeling about it. It's important to remember that a delayed reaction is no option if you feel your opponent has given a bad call. In everyday life it is often possible to react to decisions after some time has elapsed, but in a match situation you must react immediately.

GUIDELINE FOR DEALING WITH 'BAD CALLS'

1. Remember that it is essential in sport to react immediately.
2. Bear in mind that you are entitled to challenge a decision. If you know how to behave in such situations, you won't feel unsure of yourself when they occur.
3. Few people find it easy to seek a confrontation. But in this case there is no choice.
4. It is best to behave as neutrally as possible, without getting angry or raising your voice. Once again, if you have practised this, you will find it easier to apply in a stressful situation.
5. The right words to use for a challenge are 'I saw it differently, in my opinion the ball was in' or 'Can you show me where the ball bounced?'
6. In the case of a disagreement, ask for a let. Then (regardless of the outcome) there are only four productive ways in which you can react:

i. 'I handled that well, even though my opponent won't agree to a let. He'll pay more attention next time he calls a ball out. He knows that I disagreed. I'll let it go and carry on with the match.'
ii. 'Fine, we'll play a let. I'll let it go and carry on with the match.'
iii. 'I'm not accepting this; I'm going to fetch an official to bring clarity to the situation.'
iv. 'I'm only playing for pleasure and don't want to have to deal with this situation. I concede the match.'

The last alternative is certainly extreme, but we have included it so that players are aware of all their real options. Make sure that you choose one of these four reactions quite calmly, and that will always help you to quickly return to action thinking. None of the other possible reactions would benefit you in any way.

If you want to change your reactions to bad calls, try the following: Choose one or two of the guidelines given above and practise them with one of your tennis partners during a training session. Make sure that you speak clearly, without raising your voice. Keep your body language positive and calm.

If you practise this now and then, your emotions will no longer take control of you during a real match. Don't underestimate the importance of this exercise. How often does it not happen that a match is lost because of the story thinking that sets in after that 'one point'?

CHAPTER 4

LIFE VERSUS SPORT

WHAT YOU CAN'T HIDE IN SPORT

This chapter makes it clear why sport has such a strong psychological component, involving a head-on confrontation with yourself

In his autobiography, John McEnroe admits that a fear of losing was the dominant factor in virtually all his matches. He reproaches himself for the fact that throughout his illustrious career, he was hardly ever able to enjoy his victories. He says himself that he wishes he had been able to play with more enjoyment and that he envies Jimmy Connors' ability to use humour to break the tension.

One of McEnroe's best memories is the final he played against Björn Borg in New Orleans in 1979. As the tension in the match kept rising, he became more and more incensed and beside himself. At 5–5 in the third set, Borg gestured to him to come to the net. McEnroe thought to himself: 'Oh my God, what's he going to do now? Is he going to tell me I'm the biggest jerk of all time?' But Borg put his arm round him and said: 'It's okay. Just relax. It's a great match.' McEnroe says that it was such a special moment because Borg did not see his misbehaviour as a deliberate ploy to put him off his game. He saw it simply as McEnroe's own frantic state. It was the action thinker speaking to the story thinker.

What McEnroe describes is something we constantly encounter in all kinds of situations during a match. Let us look at a few subtler examples, revolving around someone we'll call 'Bob'.

Bob is having a rough time. Let's see how he behaves during a match. Few people will fail to recognize something of themselves in Bob's behaviour. But now for the surprising part: if Bob reads this book carefully and makes a serious effort to put its suggestions into practice, he can change his situation and get far more enjoyment out of his game.

Players who are underperforming often tend to blame everyone and everything except themselves. What's the explanation? It stems from the difference between fantasy and reality. If a player has a certain image of his own abilities that is not based on reality, he will find it hard to believe that his poor performance is simply attributable to himself. He will automatically search for all sorts of external causes. Bob constantly gives priority to his own fantasy rather than seeing what actually happens. He will not accept reality, and his non-acceptance leads to excuses, frustration, and an even poorer performance. But always bear in mind this one thing, a key phrase in this book: It's your game! It's up to you, and no-one else! So who or what does Bob blame when things go wrong?

Blaming someone else for not coaching

The score is 3-3, and Bob is leading 40-0. But then he hits two double faults. He casts a worried look at his girlfriend, who is watching the match, and gestures questioningly at her. She smiles at him encouragingly.

Bob loses the game, and after that his game falls apart. He loses the match, 6-3, 6-1. He marches off the court and ignores his girlfriend. 'What's wrong?' she asks. 'You don't give a damn, do you?' he explodes angrily. 'What I needed was some good coaching, not a nice smile.'

Blaming someone else for bad coaching

The score is 3-3, and Bob is leading 40-0. But then he hits two double faults. His girlfriend calls out, 'Come on, keep playing aggressively. You can do it!' and hammers an encouraging fist in the air. He casts an irritated glance in her direction.

Bob loses the game, and after that his game falls apart. He loses the match, 6-3, 6-1. His girlfriend has continued to support him throughout the match. He marches off the court and ignores her. 'What's wrong?' she asks. 'I don't want you interfering with my matches any more,' Bob explodes angrily. 'I should have been patient instead of playing more aggressively. Your bad coaching lost me the match!'

Accepting responsibility, but hating yourself

Bob leaves the court, hanging his head in shame. He couldn't even survive the first round of the tournament. He has lost 6-3, 6-1.

'I didn't hit one ball right', he fumes. 'I spent the whole match playing against myself. I was all tensed up. I really think I need therapy.'

'After the two double faults you totally choked', replies his girlfriend, who has had a miserable time watching Bob struggling with himself.

'Yes, how the hell did that happen? It was 3-3 and I was leading 40-0, then I go and hit those awful services. After that he fights back to deuce, wins the next two points and from that moment on I know I have no chance whatsoever! I'm sick of myself, I'm sick of playing matches! I'm sick of tennis altogether!'

These are examples of a recreational player. But players of all standards will be able to identify with some of these points in their own struggle.

In fact problems are even likelier to become more obvious when competing in sport than in everyday life, where it is usually possible to hide your weak points temporarily. Out on court, you'll be found out straight away. Players who are capable of developing rapid insight into their reactions, and can manage to break away from negative patterns of behaviour, will generally be able to apply the same abilities outside the court too. In other words, changing the way you compete can actually improve your life in other ways. During a match, problems that exist in your everyday life are often revealed in a concentrated form, unconcealed and blatantly obvious.

People frequently lose their self-respect while playing a match (lose their courage or nerve). Research has shown that self-respect primarily comes down to one thing. What do you do if you are faced with a difficult situation? Face it, tackle it and take action, or turn away, avoid the confrontation and let it be? In everyday life you can sometimes choose the latter course without any real consequences. But in sport it has immediate consequences, destroying your self-confidence and self-respect.

Look at the following table and try to decide which points apply to you. Don't make heavy weather of it. The aim is to shed light on the various factors that can influence what happens on a tennis court. You can easily translate the examples given here to a different sport.

	TENNIS for example, a match	LIFE for example, a work meeting
Judgment	Judgment can lead to anger/frustration or to overestimating or underestimating your opponent; this will generally have an immediate adverse effect on your game.	You think your colleague is talking nonsense. You silently pass judgment, withdraw and keep your conclusions to yourself. There are no immediate consequences.
Unrealistic self-image	Self-delusion becomes apparent within just a few minutes. When you try to hit balls that are not in your suitcase, it leads to unnecessary mistakes, causing frustration.	You constantly get involved in a discussion you know nothing about. Colleagues remain polite and you leave the meeting feeling self-satisfied.
Acceptance	If you are unable to reach a state of acceptance, for instance about your opponents' strength, the end result is frustration, which will have negative repercussions on your game.	A decision has been made that you don't accept (fewer mobile phone calls, for instance). You are very annoyed and decide inwardly to ignore it. You don't give a damn, and carry on as before.
Skills	You can't pretend to be fit or to have a good technique. If these qualities are not in your suitcase, it will immediately be obvious. The lack of these qualities will cause you to make unforced errors or lead to exhaustion, resulting in frustration.	Someone without any leadership qualities can happily stay on as the chairman of a tennis club for twenty years.
Level of attention	If you have a short attention span, it will have immediate repercussions on your game; you will lose the rally.	You spend the meeting reliving that great tennis match you played at the weekend. You occasionally nod to make it look as if you're listening.
Irritation	d will generally make you less focused, which will have immediate repercussions on your game	Peter is going on and on as always, which really gets on your nerves. You switch off and decide to make a mental shopping list until he has stopped.

Discourage-ment	When you feel discouraged, you underperform. In desperation, you may start trying to hit balls that you know perfectly well have never worked. The result is a lot of unforced errors.	You notice that you can't understand a word of what is being said and announce that you have to leave for a dentist's appointment.
Fear	Fear is immediately obvious; you choke, you can hardly lift your arm, you're not moving. This is perfectly obvious to those watching.	If you choose, you can hide your fear and it will have no immediate consequences for the meeting. At worst, your colleagues may notice sweat patches under your armpits.
Stubbornness	If your tactics don't work and you keep on stubbornly applying them all the same, you are bound to lose.	The subject of mobile phone use is on the agenda again. As a frequent caller, you always vote to allow private calls to te billed to the office. Next time your colleagues will take advantage of your absence and unanimously adopt a private calling ban.
Impatience	Impatience will immediately cost you the point.	You keep looking at your watch to see if the meeting is finally over. This is unpleasant for your colleagues, but there are no immediate consequences.

These rather unsubtle examples could be multiplied ad infinitum, but the point will be clear. When competing, weaknesses that can either be concealed or that may have no immediate consequences in everyday life, are exposed mercilessly during a match and harm your game. Of course we are not suggesting here that a lack of skill may not lead to problems at work, or that a lack of attention may not cause trouble in your relationship. The point is that during a match, unlike everyday life, weaknesses are immediately obvious and have immediate consequences. Remember that a lesson has not been learned until it has produced a change in behaviour. And that is less visible in everyday life than in sport.

You are probably starting to understand what people mean by 'coming up against yourself when competing', and what causes it. Moreover, it will now be clear why acceptance is always the first step towards progress. Remember that there is nowhere to hide during a match, and that this is one of the most important causes underlying the sense of 'powerlessness' you may have there. The transition from unconsciously incompetent to consciously incompetent marks the beginning of all progress in your game. It is a prerequisite for self-knowledge, which every player must constantly re-create.

Is conscious incompetence the same thing as 'good mistakes'?

To grow, you have to make mistakes. Sport consists of almost nothing else. Good mistakes are mistakes that are made in spite of having the right intention. Once you realize that you are not yet capable of doing something and try to change that (conscious incompetence) the change will obviously be accompanied by more mistakes than you had been making before. If you discover that you are not making any progress with your slice backhand at your present level, and want to change it into a topspin backhand, it is unavoidable that this will not work as you would like it to straight away, especially during matches.

Another example:

A player hits a deep groundstroke into a corner during a match, which his opponent cannot possibly get back. Unfortunately, the ball goes two centimetres out.

The story thinker reacts like this:

'Oh no! Now look what's happened, what bad luck! And of course it had to happen just on this important point. That point may well cost me the game. And I'm already behind! If only I had hit the ball a bit more cautiously. '

And this is how the action thinker reacts:

'The ball went exactly where I had planned, only slightly out. Bit more topspin next time.'

The ball may have gone out, but it was a 'good mistake'. The story thinker finds it frustrating, which will not do his game any good. The action thinker derives hope from it, even though he lost the point. His non-judgmental observation will actually benefit his game. It may be added that the same neutral observation is appropriate if the ball lands on the line. That does not mean that you can't derive any pleasure from a ball you hit really well. Let's look at the reactions of the story thinker and action thinker if the ball is just in.

The story thinker's reaction:

'Brilliant! What a bit of luck! And precisely on this important point. That ball might well win me this game. I hope I can hit the next ball the same way and that it doesn't go out. This next ball may well be the decisive moment in the match.'

Getting into a winning position, especially after what the story thinker calls a 'lucky break', can lead to tense, frustrating play.

The action thinker reacts very differently.

'The ball went exactly where I had planned, and landed on the line. Great! Carry on like that.'

The action thinker's reactions are much the same in the two examples, and will not disturb his mental balance in either case. This mental trans-formation can obviously not be effected overnight, but as in so many cases, the process of change starts with the realization that a different approach exists. This means that the transition has been made from 'un-conscious incompetence' to 'conscious incompetence', which is in itself an important step forwards.

At this point we want to mention an exception to the rule of always keeping strictly to non-judgmental observation. It has to do with the advantage of 'trigger-words'. At the risk of sowing confusion and in-troducing nuances that might seem to obscure rather than to clarify the issue, we feel this point must be mentioned here. A player may get an enormous kick out of a wonderful winning shot, and it will often help him to play much better. A positive response can obviously generate enthusiasm that will enhance the player's self-confidence; the point is to ensure that it does not disturb his mental balance, as in the second ex-ample of the story thinker. You will often notice high-achieving players using confidence-boosting expressions, or trigger-words, such as 'go to the ball', 'stay low', 'stay positive', and 'keep moving'. Making a fist after a great winning shot, or exchanging a 'high five' with your doubles partner, may be good ways of boosting morale. This varies from one person to the next, however. Some players will not show any sign of these confidence-boosting responses; they say their trigger-words to themselves, silently. Enthusiasm about a successful action can sometimes stir a player to start playing even better. One thing is clear, however: trigger-words have nothing to do with hoping that your opponent will make a mistake ('One more double fault and the game is mine!'). Each player will have to learn when he should 'let out' his emotions and when it is wiser to 'hold it in'. By practising this consciously in training sessions the athlete will begin to 'feel' which reaction is best suited to his character.

THE 6TH PILLAR: ACCEPTANCE

Immediate reactions are paramount in sport. There is no place for delayed reactions, excuses or passive behaviour. Whereas in everyday life you can sometimes refuse to accept things and simply muddle on, in sport this approach will spell rapid defeat.

You have already done a number of assignments to heighten your curiosity, to learn to know yourself better and to set realistic goals, and also to improve your self-discipline. These changes will eventually produce a sense of calm and will translate in the long term into self-confidence. This self-confidence will dispel tension and insecurity.

Self-confidence means being convinced that you can perform to the best of your ability, not being convinced that you will win. Performing to the best of your ability means winning the match against yourself, not against the opponent (only half of the players can win a match, but in theory you can always win from yourself). This mindset gives you the opportunity of winning twice: from yourself, and if things go well, from your opponent too. What does it mean to 'win from yourself'? You win from yourself if you set yourself realistic goals in a match and strive to achieve them. You can learn to experience this as a victory.

Pillar 6: Acceptance during sport

So, using the last five pillars, you have set yourself a number of goals for the coming period. While you're trying to achieve them, you will always experience setbacks. You may lose a match you expected to win, for instance, or sustain an injury during training. Make sure that you impress upon yourself that these losses, and even the occasional injury, may all be part of the process. And that in spite of these losses or a temporary setback as a result of an injury, you are still on the right path. If you want to improve your awareness on this front and work on these goals, use the Personal Success Plan (PSP) in chapter 9 to focus your efforts.

Pillar 6: Acceptance in everyday life

You just lost an important match, and feel that you should have won. That hurts, and you may feel unsure of yourself towards your coach. You avoid speaking to him, and actually really don't like the idea of discussing this loss. When you see your coach in your immediate surroundings, you keep right out of his way. Stop trying to avoid this confrontation. Learn to accept that even losses are best talked about, and although evaluating a win may be more fun, discussing a loss can be more useful. So rise to the challenge and don't stick your head in the sand. There's no need to be ashamed, since you did what you could at the time. Listen to what your coach has to say with an open mind, give your own opinion clearly, and write down what you consider to be the most important things to learn from the experience. Accepting disappointments instead of trying to forget about them will increase your insight and help you to make more rapid progress.

Acceptance

You always win if you accept the punches.

CHAPTER 5

ACTION THINKING: THE ART OF CONCENTRATION

WHAT KIND OF CONCENTRATION DO WE NEED WHEN?

A concrete, simple explanation of what concentration really means, and of how players can train their own powers of concentration.

The inner calm and relaxed attitude to which Roger Federer attributes his success is something we would all like to achieve. What is it that often holds us back? Fear. Fear of losing, fear of overhitting the ball, fear that our abilities will let us down. We can all remember times when our thoughts started 'racing like crazy'. How fantastic it would be to be able to calm them. If we can achieve the right sort of concentration, the 'wild monkey' will disappear from our minds.

Concentration

To perform well in any sport, nothing matters more than concentration. In sports terminology, it is often called 'attention control'. Achieving the right kind of concentration is essential. Just as practising technique will improve your strokes, it's also possible to train your ability to concentrate. Everyone knows that your game goes downhill immediately with even the smallest lapse of concentration. The result is unforced errors. On the other hand, we also often hear references to 'over-concentration'. We would argue that no such thing exists. Later on in this chapter, it will become clear why 'over-concentration' is the wrong term: you can't concentrate too much, the point is that you might be concentrating on the wrong thing.

If a player achieves the right kind of concentration in a match, you always hear the same kind of comments afterwards, which all have to do with action thinking: 'it all went automatically', 'I didn't have to think', 'I was totally absorbed in the moment (= the now)', 'I was completely immersed in the game', and so on. Story thinking leads you away from where your attention ought to be, in the here and now. Action thinking takes you to the point where all your attention is needed. When you have achieved perfect concentration, there are no distractions left beyond the game. You can learn to conjure up this concentration by practising it specifically as you do technique.

The sports psychologist Robert Nideffer has done pioneering research in this field. The publication in 1976 of his book *Attention control training* was a milestone in research on attention control. We have developed our own approach to concentration, which is partly inspired by Nideffer.

Our method in sport is based on four different types of concentration: scan and zoom are **external concentration**, your attention focuses on the outside world: your opponent, the weather, the ball, and so on. This concentration is visual. Thought and feeling are **internal concentration**, your attention is focused on your 'inner world': thoughts, feelings and sensory experiences. This includes visualizing a rally, the tactics you have decided on, and bodily awareness (breathing, muscle tension et cetera).

Sports people are constantly switching between the four categories of concentration: **feeling** (internal), **thought** (internal), **zooming** (narrow-visual) and **scanning** (wide-visual).

Four concentrations	Type
scan	external wide visual
zoom	external narrow visual
thought	internal
feeling	internal

Here are a few examples to clarify what we mean

Someone looking at a group of horses standing in a meadow **scans** the whole area (external wide visual).

If he looks at the brush he is using to groom a horse, he **zooms** in (external narrow visual).

If he thinks of a plan for getting the horses into the stable efficiently, he allows his **thoughts** to range freely (internal).

From a familiar **feeling** (internal) he will make certain noises that always help to calm the horses and make it easy to move them.

How do you recognize the different kinds of concentration?

Perhaps it will help if you recall that you are constantly switching between scanning, zooming, thought and feeling all the time in everyday life. Take a situation in which you are cycling through town.

- You constantly have to pay attention to the road surface immediately ahead to check for direct obstacles or holes in the road. That is **zooming**.
- You also have to pay attention to the traffic situation (is the next side-road a one-way street? Is the traffic light up ahead red, is the parked car moving out?). That is **scanning**.
- Having looked well, both scanning and zooming, you decide to speed up, since the light is still green. That is strategy: **thought**.
- Then you let your muscles take over, you accelerate your leg action and enjoy the sensation of racing and of wind in your hair. That is **feeling**.

Is it possible for a player to consciously train concentration and to train shifting attention from one category to another?

It is not only possible to train concentration, it is fun and easy. Four simple exercises to clarify these differences. If you do these exercises, you will immediately feel what is meant by each of the different categories. They are exercises in the four different categories of concentration. By doing these exercises you are training your mind.

Exercise 1: Zoom

Try to REALLY follow the ball from a) to f), in each separate rally.

a. your point of impact with the ball / where exactly does the ball hit the strings on your racket
b. the ball's path after it leaves your racket (rotation, height, speed)
c. the bounce on the other side of the net
d. your opponent's point of impact with the ball / where exactly does the ball hit the strings of the opponent's racket
e. the ball's return path
f. the bounce on your side

When the rally is over, look at the strings of your racket or your shoelaces (as did Björn Borg); that is how you keep your focus on zooming.

Exercise 2: Scan

Try to remain constantly aware of your opponent's position and the open space in the court for a full three minutes. In this exercise, focusing on the ball is of secondary importance (easier to practise in a one-to-one situation on the singles court).

a. Where is your opponent in relation to the baseline?
b. Where is your opponent in relation to the sidelines?
c. Where is most space to hit the ball?
d. Where are you standing in relation to the baseline?
e. Where are you standing in relation to the sidelines?
f. Where are you standing in relation to your opponent?
g. Where are you standing in relation to the ball you hit?

Exercise 3: Feeling

Feeling will be clarified in chapter 6 where we explain the importance of bodily awareness through the use of instruments. But to start you off on the right track do the following exercises:

Try to remain aware of how tightly you are holding your racket for a full three minutes. How does the tension in your hand feel? Are you squeezing the racket handle or are you holding it loosely? Feel your muscle tension in your hand in all the following situations:

a. while preparing to hit the ball
b. at the moment of impact
c. when following through with your racket
d. when the ball is on the other side
e. in between points.

Repeat the above, but now pay attention to a. your shoulder muscles, b. your breath.

Exercise 4: Thought

You have already been training the concentration form 'thought' by using the six pillars and working on the assignments. As explained earlier, without action thinking (a balanced mind) a player is not capable of making clear and efficient tactical decisions.

Try the following during a practice match. Normally you play a match in a tactical way that suits you. Now try making a drastic change to the way you play (tactics) for once. Try a new pattern of play against a familiar opponent, for instance by hitting every ball cross-court (without mentioning it beforehand). Or by taking every short ball as an approach shot and going to the net. Take note of the effect caused by these new tactics.

By doing exercises of this kind regularly, you will gradually find that it starts to go automatically. You will become more and more familiar with the different kinds of concentration. One important element that is easy to train is switching between scanning and zooming. This switch will eventually become automatic, and it will become easy to find the right kind of concentration for each moment of play. As a result, you will anticipate better, and gain insight into position play and tactics. You will also acquire more self-confidence.

As you see in the charts on the following two pages, the four concentrations and the instruments (chapter 6) may be either positive or negative in their effect. Do you use the concentration of a story thinker or an action thinker?

STORY THINKING

SCAN

Distracted by:
- Spectators
- Another court
- Moving objects other than the ball
- Difficult weather

FEELING

1. Negative
2. Uncertain
3. Giving up
4. Impatient
5. Hesitant
6. Listless
7. Stubborn
8. Fearful
9. Predictable
10. Dependent
11. Distracted

ZOOM

Distracted by:
- Opponent: arrogant, irritating, overwhelming
- Clothes / rackets
- Coach / parent / spectators
- Facial expression; agressive, unfriendly, off-putting
- Body language: way of counting, swearing
- Opponent's comments
- Bad bounces

INSTRUMENTS

1. Negative trigger-words
2. Haunting images
3. Rushed / irregular breath
4. Paralysed
5. Restless
6. Rushed or no rituals
7. Distracted eyes
8. Distracting sounds
9. Noise in your head

THOUGHT

Past and future
Judgmental
Hostile
Too many thoughts
Irrational

WHAT DO YOU

ACTION THINKING

SCAN

Focused on:
- Opponent's position
- Opening in the court
- 'Mirroring' your position in the court
- Surface of the court
- Weather conditions

FEELING

1. Positive
2. Self-confident
3. Perseverant
4. Patient
5. With conviction
6. Motivated
7. Flexible
8. Courageous
9. Creative
10. Autonomous
11. Focused

ZOOM

Focused on:
- The ball
  spin, direction, height, speed, depth
- Opponent
  grip, shoulders, position of feet, angle of racket
- Coach/parent/partner for encouragement
- Opponent's body language (physical and emotional state)
- Racket strings

INSTRUMENTS

1. Trigger-words
2. Visualization
3. Breathing
4. Movement & heartbeat
5. Recovery
6. Rituals
7. Eye control
8. Sound
9. Inner music

THOUGHT

Present
Non-judgmental
Observant
Tactics:
Clear and decisive

CONCENTRATE ON?

What causes unforced errors?

As you see in the charts, scanning and zooming are visual. This means, roughly speaking, that you know when to focus on the ball with your eyes, that you see how your opponent is approaching the ball, and that you also see where your opponent is, and where there is an opening in the court. This focus has to do with your observation of the outside world. By far the most important kind of concentration in sport is the ability to switch from zooming to scanning and vice versa. If you stay fixated on one for too long, this will immediately cause an unforced error. That is because your timing will no longer be right because of poorer anticipation / observation, as a result of which you have a lapse of concentration and miss the ball. Poor switching can also cause you to be out of position or not ready for the ball. Often scanning and zooming are disturbed by thought. By becoming aware of this you will be able tot train them and notice immediate improvement.

Where should my concentration be at the beginning of a point?

In general, in relation to the serve and return of serve, the following order applies. This is also true for other disciplines, for example a corner in soccer or hockey:

1. decide where you are going to place the ball **(thought)**
2. visualize your target **(feeling)**
3. start your rituals, for instance bouncing the ball, holding the racket loosely **(feeling)**
4. When serving: focus on the ball until the point of impact, then continue to focus on the ball until the opponent's point of impact **(zoom)** When receiving: focus on the ball from the server's hand until the point of impact. Continue to follow the ball until your own point of impact **(zoom)**

As soon as you start to toss the ball to serve, your concentration consists of zooming; after that you constantly switch between scanning and zooming. Let's take an example: you decide that you are going to serve wide (thought). This is a very brief, fast and simple thought that takes about two seconds. Then you focus on your breathing and visualize where you intend to place the ball (feeling). Then come your familiar rituals (feeling). Then you briefly look at (scan) the service box, both to get a clear picture of where you want to place the ball and to establish your opponent's position. You start to toss the ball, and then your concentration shifts to zooming in on the ball. For the return of serve, everything is exactly the same, with one exception: you follow your opponent's tossing arm and the ball in his hand when you switch to the visual.

Where do things go wrong, and why?

> The most common mistake is switching immediately from thought to scanning and zooming, without using the necessary 'bridge' of feeling (bodily awareness).

Many players, of all standards, control their 'zoom' with 'thought'. They miss out the concentration form of feeling. This is the wrong approach, because thoughts are conscious, while the action in a rally takes place at the level of unconscious or automatic response. This can only work if thoughts switch to the scanning and zooming by way of feeling.

Let's look at an example. Players often remain fixated on thoughts about tactics after they have lost a point. 'I must play to his backhand, otherwise he will seize the initiative!' In itself this may be a good idea, but not if the player then switches straight to scanning and zooming, and not if the thought lasts too long; then it becomes part of story thinking. The right way to control your play is: use the concentration form feeling to go to scanning and zooming. The concentration that is needed to achieve the best action while playing a rally cannot be directly controlled by concern or thoughts about tactics. Here in the following chart an example of how the concentrations work during play.

	Zoom	Scan	Feeling	Thought
Action thinking	Correct estimation of opponent's topspin	Playing the ball in the open corner	Shaking off muscular tension, moving your racket to the other hand, keeping moving to get rid of tension	Using the changeover to think of the right tactics and taking time to reach your feeling
Story thinking	Incorrect estimation of opponent's topspin (attention was not focused on racket face and ball at the opponent's moment of impact)	Playing the ball to your opponent	Keeping your muscles constantly tensed up. Squeezing the racket.	Thinking about irrelevant things during the changeover. Not taking enough time, and focusing only on what went wrong instead of thinking of the right tactics

What is anticipation and how can I improve it?

Anticipation consists of scanning and zooming. So without actually using the word 'anticipation', we have already written a great deal about it. Anticipation is actually much easier than the average player thinks; many people assume that it is a really tricky skill to acquire. It is very rare for specific training sessions to be devoted to it. In fact anticipation really just means 'looking specifically and carefully'. Whilst developing the Mindset approach, 100% of the participants said that the scan and zoom exercises had a) helped them to acquire more insight into what anticipation really meant, and b) helped them to improve their anticipation, in a single day. What would this mean if you were to practise these skills specifically on a daily basis?

What should you focus your attention on? If you regularly zoom in on your opponent's hips and shoulders just before he hits the ball, you will find that you can tell at a very early stage the direction in which the ball is going to go. The same applies to zooming in on the position of the feet. The grip, racket-head and swing also reveal a lot of information, as does the speed with which your opponent rotates his body.

Situation anticipation (recognizing certain patterns that your opponent uses repeatedly) and improving your assessment of situations during play involve a different range of skills. It takes a great many hours of training and match-playing to learn to recognize patterns of this kind.

How should I start a match?

When you walk into the sporting arena, you observe the weather conditions or lighting and other relevant matters: for instance, are there net-posts, where is the broom (it might be an obstacle), is there a chair, is the net at the right height? You have to make sure that anything that might distract your attention is immediately dealt with. Your concentration consists of scanning. You make sure that you feel comfortable with the situation and that there is nothing niggling you. Don't underestimate this point. This stage lays the foundations for your self-confidence. Let's assume that you do not know your opponent (otherwise you will already have a game plan). In the first two minutes of warming-up you start by scanning and zooming; then you switch to thought (tactics); you try to obtain information about your opponent. Does he or she have weak points? If you concentrate properly (scan and zoom) during the warming up, you will be able to detect the strengths and weaknesses of your opponent with relative ease. What tactics do you plan to use? Then your attention shifts to feeling: you try to get into the relaxed and familiar feeling of hitting the ball well; at the same time you visualize your regular game plan or the tactics you have thought up, based on the information you have found out about your opponent.

Where should my concentration be during and after the points in a match?

As soon as the match begins, all your concentration switches to the visual. You play in the expectation that what you have prepared with feeling and thought, can now be carried out by your body. Throughout the match scanning, zooming and feeling are the main concentration forms. In between points you briefly switch to thought, to adjust or maintain your tactics; then all your attention switches to the instruments (see next chapter) that produce the right feeling.

When you are going to work, you make a plan for what you are going to do that day, you are 'at the office'. The same applies to sport. Before the match you decide what game plan to use, and during the match you constantly evaluate that game plan when changing sides (thought) and adjust it when necessary. Since this situation is not very different from one that you might have at your work, we call it 'at the office'. This is the only time when it makes sense to spend more than about five seconds in the realm of thought, provided that it does not turn into story thinking. We mean by this that clear tactical decisions are taken, not that your thoughts begin to lead a life of their own.

At the office (change-over)

What happens to your concentration during the changeover / at the office? The thoughts of action thinking play a very important role here. The following is a description of the kind of concentration needed during the change-over:

1. Always sit down during the changeover. The changeover is for thinking and drinking! *Feeling*
2. Start by relaxing, have a drink, wipe your sweat off and sit down, trying to feel alert but relaxed. Make sure that you drink enough, since it has been scientifically proven that fluid loss leads to a significant loss of concentration. *Feeling*
3. Focus on regulating your breathing. *Feeling*
4. When you are sure that your body is relaxed, and not before then, start thinking if you need to change your tactics in any way. Consider whether your tactics have worked up to now. If they have not, try to pin down why, and what changes need to be made. *Thought*
5. In a doubles match, analyze the games you have just played, together with your partner, and decide whether your tactics need to be maintained, modified slightly, or changed altogether. *Thought*
6. Close your eyes and visualize your tactics. *Feeling*
7. Pick up your racket, enjoy the sensation of movement in your body, walk out onto your side of the court with a confident step. *Feeling*
8. Say a brief trigger-word, speaking it out loud if you want, to create the right kind of energy within yourself. *Feeling*

How can you correct the wrong kind of concentration?

If you find yourself in the negative concentration of story thinking (as described in the first concentration chart), there is only one way to change it: swith your concentration to the second chart, to action thinking. The action thinking chart corrects the story thinking chart.

Of course we are well aware how difficult and complex this may be at times. 'Story thinking' constantly impinges on you, because it is part of your personality. Still, it is easier than you think. Let's look at four examples illustrating how you can apply a positive correction to the wrong kind of concentration:

SCAN: If you are distracted by a spectator, focus your attention on your opponent's position.

ZOOM: If you are intimidated by your opponent's appearance (for instance because he or she is tall and strong), focus on the rotation of his or her hips, to help you anticipate the path of the ball.

FEELING: If fear is making it impossible for you to relax and play freely, use movement to loosen up your muscles, and then use your rituals to stay in the 'now'.

THOUGHT: If you are distracted by negative thoughts, switch to feasible tactics, linked to a realistic view of your own abilities. Don't base your tactics on judgment but on scanning and zooming, which will enable you to observe exactly what you have to do and shift to action thinking.

What is the ideal kind of concentration?

When a player is 'in the zone', his concentration is purely visual (external) and he constantly switches back and forth between scanning and zooming. This happens automatically. The more easily a player can switch between scanning and zooming, the better his concentration is. Only in the brief periods in between points does his concentration shift to thoughts or feeling (internal). Monica Seles, who was ranked number 1 in the world for 178 weeks in a row in the 1990s and won nine grand slam tournaments, once made an interesting comment in an interview. She said that she was constantly in the zone when playing her best tennis, but that 'once you think about being in the zone, you are immediately out of it'.

That means that you can only get into the zone if your concentration is in the visual, and that you switch in between points from feeling and not from thought. The demands of technique and tactics are met automatically. As soon as your concentration shifts to judgmental thoughts ('Oh, I'm playing so fantastically now, I hope I can keep it up'), you lose the flow, because you slip back into story thinking.

The non-concept of 'over-concentration'

Now let's return to the non-concept of 'over-concentration', which we mentioned at the beginning of this chapter. All four categories of attention have to be deployed at the right time. If you linger in one of them for too long, your concentration will lapse. That does not mean that you are 'over-concentrated', but that you have not switched in time to the correct focus. As soon as you become aware of this, you will no longer have to struggle with the confusing and nonsensical concept of 'over-concentration', but will see that you have simply stayed focused on the wrong thing for too long.

Top players train scanning and zooming
before even stepping on court

When Martina Navratilova reached forty, she noticed her focus was far from optimal at the beginning of matches. She took to playing with a tennis ball for 20 minutes before the beginning of each match, bouncing it and in this way teaching the pupil of her eye to achieve the maximum concentration. In our terms, she chose to practise 'zooming'.

Andy Murray often plays a football match against his coaches, but using a tennis ball. The rules are: one bounce, both feet can be used and the ball must bounce in the service box. This activates almost everything that is needed for a match in a fun way: scanning, zooming and feeling, making quick decisions, playing points, movement and agility and accurate footwork. All this without wearing himself out. This is a great way to warm up physically and mentally, try it!

ASSIGNMENTS TO IMPROVE CONCENTRATION

1. When beginning a training, always start by heightening your concentration. Do this by using the exercises for scanning, zooming and feeling described in this chapter. Do not train 'thought' in the warming up as in everyday life our thoughts are continually rattling on, it is now time to calm them. Scanning, zooming and feeling are the concentration forms that you should use to achieve this so that you begin every training in action thinking.

2. a. Which of the four types of concentration are you best at during a match? Thought, feeling, zooming or scanning?
   b. Write down the specific qualities that you possess within your chosen form of concentration. Use the action thinking table in this chapter to help choose your answers.

3. a. Which of the four types of concentration do you think you should work on? Thought, feeling, zooming or scanning?
   b. Write down clearly and specifically what you want to improve in your concentration.
   Look at the story thinking table in this chapter to help choose your answers.

Ask your coach or another player whether it would be possible to work on the chosen form of concentration, so that you can learn to focus better during matches.

CHAPTER 6

STORY THINKING: HOW DO YOU ESCAPE FROM IT?

INSTRUMENTS TO ACHIEVE THE RIGHT FEELING

The practical application to be able to play every match with self-confidence and clear focus. The magic key to achieving these goals is emotional balance. At the start of every rally or action, the athlete must use the concentration form feeling. There are nine instruments to help you find that feeling.

In chapter 1 we wrote that everyone can achieve the following things:

1. To play freely in a match instead of tensing up.
2. Not to have to fight against yourself during a match.
3. To feel acceptance and self-confidence instead of frustration about your game.
4. Not to feel irritated by your opponent.
5. To transform your fear of failure into faith in yourself and self-confidence.
6. To know how best to focus/concentrate, both in training sessions and in matches.
7. To change the 'battlefield' feeling into a 'playing field' feeling.

The following instruments will help bring you in the concentration form feeling. Bodily awareness will be perfect before the point commences. Thoughts will diminish and the malfunctioning machine of story thinking will be conquered by mindfulness of action thinking.

1. Trigger-words
2. Visualization
3. Breathing
4. Movement / heartbeat
5. Recovery
6. Rituals
7. Eye control
8. Sound
9. Inner music

We want to repeat that you can't achieve the right kind of concentration if you switch directly from thoughts and/or negative feelings to zooming and scanning. This is the most important mistake made by athletes at every level. When your emotions take control of your game, you can turn this around by using the instruments listed above to balance your mind. You use instruments and the six pillars to neutralize your emotions and bring you in the feeling of action thinking. The chart below represents the differences in concentration between the two mindsets.
On the left hand side you see that thought in story thinking takes up all your minds energy and time. This leaves less space for scanning, zooming and feeling. On the right hand side you see that in action thinking, scanning and zooming get more space because feeling is emphasized, not thought. In this way thoughts of action thinking are short, clear and tactical.

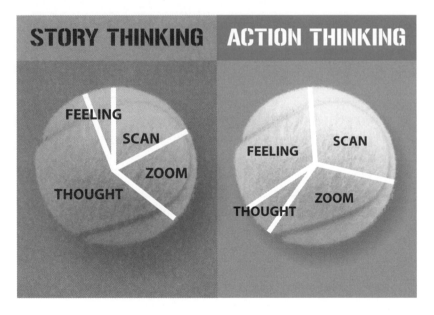

In the following pages, we present a systematic approach that can help you eliminate frustration, anger, tension, the fear of failure and a sense of helplessness during a match and to break through negative patterns.

Athletes often 'know' that these are important issues, and yet fail to deal with them because they have not really come to grips with them and they have remained purely theoretical ideas. What is more, 'rational' thinking often wins from intuition. You know that you must change, you even know how… but you can't bring yourself to do it (you are controlled by story thinking). So what is the formula for breaking this impasse and reaching an attitude that reflects the 'light side' of action thinking? The answer is simple: by training MENTAL skills. Focus your attention specifically on training the four concentrations, the six pillars and the nine instruments instead of technique or tactics. It is not complicated; the method is consistently simple, tangible and practical.

THE NINE INSTRUMENTS

1. Trigger-words

What are trigger-words?
Trigger-words are one or two words that you repeat to produce a positive influence on your actions. Some people like to write them down, so as to be constantly reminded of them. Others prefer to say them, either silently or out loud.

Trigger-words and 'priming'
The social psychologist John Bargh made a study of 'automaticity', the ability to perform a task without your mind having to concern itself with all sorts of minor details that are involved in that task. Other psychologists had called this mental process 'mindless', but Bargh claimed that the processes involved were not mindless but unconscious or 'automatic'.

An interesting part of his research was a study of 'priming', in which subjects in one group were required to perform a task with a lot of synonyms for elderly people such as 'old', 'grey' or 'forgetful'. The other group was not 'primed' with these words. After this task, the subjects were asked to go to a different room. The astonishing thing was that the first group displayed signs of old age: they walked noticeably more slowly than the other group.

If you give one group of players an assignment and add terms of encouragement ('you will certainly be able to do this'), and give another group the same assignment with a more discouraging message ('this is something that everyone finds really difficult'), the first group will adopt a different attitude and will learn the task more quickly and satisfactorily.

The idea behind 'priming' is that you can influence behaviour by the words you use. And this explains how trigger-words work in sport. Trigger-words influence behaviour far more effectively than long-winded instructions, because they set in motion automatic, unconscious processes. By doing so, they prevent you from slipping into story thinking. In the 2007 final at Roland Garros, when Justine Henin was leading by 4–1 in the first set, she took a closed envelop out of her tennis bag and tore it open. It contained a note with trigger-words in capital letters: 'COURIR, COURIR, COURIR' ('RUN RUN RUN'). You may be thinking, 'What a load of rubbish!', but the world number one was aware that even she might lose her way and stiffen up. She refreshed herself mentally by heightening her bodily awareness with the simple device of a few trigger-words. She did it again when she was leading 6–1, 5–2. Even with this enormous lead, at which point most players would be thinking that the match is in the bag, or getting nervous that they might not be able to finish it off, she was using trigger-words. She won the match from Ana Ivanovic, who had completely lost her way and whose face showed signs of despair at the final changeover. Perhaps a trigger-word might have helped her to recover and to escape from the story thinking that clearly had her in its clutches.

Trigger-words and story thinking

Negative 'self-talk' undermines self-confidence and leads to frustration. It is the most visible example of the negative effects of story thinking. But what about positive self-talk? You might think that this too is a kind of story thinking. It is true that positive self-talk consisting of a lengthy discourse doesn't work at all. It may get you stuck into story thinking. 'Wow, you tackled that brilliantly in that rally, and that volley with which you clinched the point was hit perfectly: a few more strokes like that and the set will be mine!' That belongs in the category of story thinking and is not helpful.

Positive self-talk should consist of short exclamations – what we call 'trigger-words'. The emphasis is on what you do want to achieve (your goals) and not on what you don't want to do. A clear instruction that leads to positive physical action. Short words that can immediately be translated into action. 'Not so fast!' or 'don't do that!' are meaningless and seldom have any effect. Useful trigger-words are 'Come on, go to the ball!', 'take it early!', 'stay low!' or 'keep the initiative!'. It may also be useful to say 'it's o.k.' after a miss-hit, because it prevents negative emotions cropping up. If you miss a ball as a result of a terrific action by your opponent, say 'good shot!' or make an 'applause' gesture with your racket. This takes the pressure off a little, and ensures that you will start the next point with a positive mindset. Acknowledging great play by your opponent gives you space and releases pressure. Even so, it is unwise to praise your opponent's winning shots all too often. It will increase his self-confidence and it may make you feel like the lesser player. Use praise only for a really exceptional shot.

At the highest level, people seldom compliment each other on their play; many players and coaches claim it 'helps' your opponent. Fortunately the new generation of players, including Roddick, Federer, Nadal, Ivanovic and Dementieva, are showing us a different face of sportsmanship.

Fists, notes and mantras

Trigger-words are a way of keeping yourself alert. They introduce a kind of structured courage into your game. You could also say that by saying something intentionally out loud, you trigger the subconscious. You will notice that Rafael Nadal, for instance, constantly makes the same gestures and always uses the same word ('Vamos!') to rouse himself after winning a point. Again: we do not claim that everyone should do this as explicitly as Nadal. We are merely showing how trigger-words work. Roger Federer and Pete Sampras are examples of self-possessed players who have different, more internal, positive performance triggers. The way that works best for you will depend on your personality. But never underestimate the power of words.

It is interesting to compare trigger-words to mantras. A mantra is a word or expression that is repeated constantly during meditation. It is used to transport the person concerned into the here and now. Meditation can help you to stop identifying with the emotions and thoughts of the past and future, as a result of which you are less likely to become distracted. In the present context, we might say that a mantra helps to banish story thinking and heightens alertness. And that is what mantras and trigger-words have in common: they transport you to the here and now and enhance your mindfulness.

2. Visualization

Visualization is the link between the mental and the physical. It is the best manner to overcome fear. You learn to face fear, greet it as a known friend and replace it with the feeling that you would prefer to have under pressure. That's why it is so important. Visualizing means conjuring up pictures of situations and of the way in which you will respond and act in those situations. It is thinking in images. Professional sportsmen and sportswomen often visualize their actions beforehand. In a survey of Olympic coaches and international athletes in a wide range of sports, the respondents were asked to identify the most important element of their mental training programmes. Without exception, 'visualization' came at the top of the list. One popular slogan is 'If you can see it, you can do it'.

Visualization extends beyond the game itself, you can practise it daily. Navratilova says that athletes forget to visualize their emotions. She claims that you can learn to deal with the tension of a match by evoking the emotions that can be produced during a match again and again. If you deliberately conjure up fears, they become familiar to you and you learn to recognize them more quickly. You then replace these emotions with the way you would like to feel, the next time that the situation arises. As a result, you will eventually be able to conquer your fears when they arise during a match.

Try to visualize instead of verbalizing. Don't allow story thinking to take possession of you: to fight it off, turn your attention inward and picture to yourself what you are going to do with the ball. Just doing this will in itself help to relax you. Picture how the next rally will go. Visualization helps to shift you into action thinking. It stimulates the part of your brain that controls automatic processes – the opposite of analytical processes – and wards off the syndrome of 'paralysis by analysis'.

You know more about visualization than you think

Everyone who likes sport enjoys watching matches on the television. How does it actually affect you? The next time you practice, you suddenly notice a difference in your game: everything is going 'automatically'. Apparently, the images have done something to your body. Even the most inexperienced of players have discovered that visualization can have a tangible impact on their game. You see yourself hitting balls just like your hero in yesterday's grand slam final. By watching the world's best players in action, you form a picture of the various strokes. Visualization can really help you to progress when you start practising your strokes or playing a match.

In what situations is visualization easy to apply?

When waiting to return serve, you should always picture to yourself where you are going to hit the ball. Regardless of whether the ball comes to your forehand or backhand, you should form a clear mental image of the part of the court where you want to place the ball. The same applies to the first and second serve. Many players retort, 'But I just can't place my serve accurately at all!' To those people, we would say, 'But have you ever put any effort into trying to do so?' With enough effort and determination, anyone can succeed in placing their serve. To test the truth of this remark, go out onto the court, place two target objects in the corners of the service box, and practise. You will be pleasantly surprised by the result!

And we want to repeat: when playing a rally in a match, don't think of all sorts of technical things like your grip, the angle of your racket-face, the position of your body. All these things have been stored in your subconscious by your training sessions. Try to picture to yourself your movement and the path of the ball. It sometimes helps to briefly close your eyes. Another thing that may make visualization easier is deploying several senses at once: for instance hearing (the 'plock' sound made by the ball, the 'singing' of the racket-strings), touch (the feel of the stroke) and smell (the clay, the ball).

Practising visualization

One great thing about visualization is that you can practise it anywhere: even sitting at home, at the office, or on the beach. A good exercise is to think of the strongest and weakest points of your game, and then to work on them in a virtual training session. For instance, if your volley is not so strong, or your lobs tend to go out, try to picture to yourself as well as possible (as well as to feel, hear et cetera) what it is like to hit a perfect volley, or a lob that lands just inside the baseline. Remember to see and acknowledge the mistake and the negative emotions first. If you realize that it might go wrong again, but you know how to correct it, nerves will not take hold of you when a tense moment arises in a match. It is best to do this a few times a week. You will see that it gradually becomes easier and that your game improves when you are on court, just as it does after a physical training session that focuses on an aspect of technique. Try to spend a few minutes before the start of a match or training session visualizing the strokes you want to execute, and then another few minutes when it's finished, visualizing those you want to improve next time. And while actually training or playing a match, visualize for a few seconds before each rally; you obviously have a little more time in the changeover during matches. You will find that it eventually becomes a routine that helps you.

An important point: when you hit a ball badly, you should try to banish any memory of it immediately, and visualize yourself hitting it perfectly instead. You will often see professional players turning around immediately after a mistake and walking away, to forget the stroke as quickly as possible. Frequently they will mimic the action that they wanted to perform, without the ball. They do this so that the next time this situation occurs, they will be able to evoke the correct memory from their feeling instead of repeating the unforced mistake. Conversely, if you make a fantastic winning shot, keep looking towards the ball and savour the stroke for a few seconds, so that the action remains indelibly printed in your memory.

3. Breathing and pranayama

Breathing is the most important factor when it comes to regulating match tension. Irregularity of the breath is the first sign of story thinking.

The quicker a player becomes aware of irregularities in his breathing, the quicker he realises that story thinking is looming.

As soon as you focus your attention on breathing, you step out of story thinking and automatically shift to the here and now of action thinking. Past and future disappear, and you are in direct contact with your body. Focusing on breathing is key to most forms of meditation: the flow of thoughts and emotions is interrupted, with the objective of attaining 'full presence'. In Buddhism, this state is referred to as selflessness or 'pure awareness'. In a match, focusing attention on your breathing will help to boost your concentration to the maximum.

Breathing exercises or pranayama have been at the heart of Eastern methods of meditation for thousands of years. Pranayama is a Sanskrit word made up of the words for control (yama) and life force (prana), and embraces a range of breathing exercises that help you to banish tension from your body and to achieve a tranquil state of mind. Its techniques empty your mind of thoughts and calm the ego. A well-known technique that is used to calm the mind and to gain control of our emotions is holding your breath after exhaling. This technique enables you to switch from story to action thinking. It is striking that this device is not widely applied in the sporting world, in particular during the changeover. We are convinced that it could make a very useful contribution to reducing the tension that arises in matches. Try it now and feel what happens.

Practising breathing
During the changeover:
- breathe through your nose;
- push your belly out when inhaling; this way you know you are breathing deeply;
- say 'five' when exhaling, and then, counting down, say 'four' the next time you exhale, down to 'one'.

This technique helps to break down lactic acid in your body, it ensures that your brain is well supplied with oxygen, and helps you to focus on the 'now'. You achieve the right concentration (feeling) and learn to gain control of your nerves and to prevent 'choking'.

During points:

A player who is in balance breathes out at the moment of impact. Just as in numerous martial arts, it is necessary to expel air with a strong impulse or gasp at that moment in order to get more strength out of your muscles. Just by making that sound, you will know that you are breathing out (you can't gasp while breathing in).

If you are performing well, you don't need to pay attention to breathing; it will automatically be working well. But if you feel a little listless and find it hard to focus, speed up your breathing to achieve a higher energy level. Conversely, if you are too hyped up, try to slow your breathing down. Deep, long and regular breathing will help you find your balance. The exercises that are described above will help to achieve this. The mere fact that your attention is focused on breathing will help to banish story thinking from your mind and to achieve emotional balance.

N.B. If you continue to find it hard to regulate your breathing, we would advise you to consult an expert.

4. Movement and its relationship with heartbeat

Movement is an absolute prerequisite for remaining alert and relaxed at the same time. Most recreational players move far too little during matches. It is well known that even at the highest level, players sometimes move far too little as a result of fear and match tension. Players often assume a static pose in between rallies. This happens most frequently when players allow their minds to get bogged down in story thinking. That makes it almost impossible to go from thoughts to the instruction 'move!' and then to the feeling of 'movement'. Players often want to 'command and compel' themselves to move instead of 'feeling' their bodies and guiding themselves with 'friendly eyes' and self-respect. If you keep moving, it will increase your energy to the level you need to achieve the right kind of concentration; this process has to become internalized, automatic.

If you keep moving it directly affects your heartbeat. Like breathing, your heartbeat is an excellent indicator of your energy level. Both breathing and heartbeat can be regulated. If you notice that your heartbeat is too fast, you can slow it down, do this by taking a longer recovery time and breathing more deeply. You are allowed a recovery time of twenty seconds in between points. Many players fail to take advantage of this. It is the ideal time to concentrate on feeling. If your heartbeat is too slow, it will help you to achieve the right energy level to keep moving actively. From competitive levels onward, a normal heartbeat would be around 100 to 120 a minute between points, while during a rally it often reaches 180. For recreational players, the heartbeat in between points and the speed of recovery depend greatly on stamina and age. Your heartbeat / stamina is linked to the capacity to achieve mental calm. If your body cannot recover well and rapidly, escaping from story thinking becomes far more difficult. If you pay attention to your heartbeat more frequently and more consciously, you can learn to constantly maintain the necessary physical and mental alertness during a match or training session. This is assuming, of course, that your basic level of fitness is satisfactory.

5. Recovery

Without a good understanding of what recovery is and how it works, you will find that much of the match passes you by. Making conscious use of recovery time is crucial to being totally focused at the start of each new rally. Don't start a point until you feel that you are mentally ready and bodily aware. This is a priceless habit. Steffi Graf had a reputation for 'acceleration'; her preference was for an average recovery time of just 10 seconds, enabling her to disrupt the rhythm of numerous opponents. Rafael Nadal is the opposite. Since he always takes a 20-second break (sometimes as much as 45 seconds!) in between points, his opponent may find himself in danger of lapsing into story thinking.

Don't start the point until you feel that your heartbeat indicates that you are ready and you have visualized what you are going to do. Make sure that you have a proper recovery moment after every point, the length of time spent on your recovery, also depends on the amount of effort you put into the point before.

In general, when a match gets exciting, or when a point has been tightly contested, players tend to be in too much of a rush to start the next rally. Have you noticed how often it happens that, after having played a brilliant point, you immediately follow it up by making an unforced error? That happens because you have taken too little recovery time to produce the right feeling. If you are satisfied with the way a match is going, you may consider deliberately taking only a brief recovery time.

This will generally benefit you in this case and put your opponent at a disadvantage.

It often feels good to keep returning between rallies to a place on the court that you can see as a 'safe haven', for instance far behind the baseline. Take the time to pick up the balls and to prepare to serve. If your muscles feel tense, flex them briefly and then relax them. It helps to let your arms and hands to hang down loosely and to 'shake them out'. This gets rid of tension in your muscles. You can do the same with your legs.

Don't forget to move your racket to your other hand during your recovery time. It gives your active arm a moment of rest.

It should be noted that in official matches, the maximum break between points is 20 seconds, and at the changeover 90 seconds.

6. Rituals

Rituals transport you to the 'now' and create a sense of security. They are the final step towards producing the right feeling for the beginning of play. That is why they are so important and should not be underestimated. You could qualify them as dynamic meditation. Rituals are fixed patterns of behaviour in between points and before points, used to achieve the right kind of concentration and relaxation. It is this bodily awareness that makes the difference between top athletes and sub-toppers.

Let's look at a few striking examples: neither Nadal nor Baghdatis will ever tread on the lines when walking back onto court after the changeover; this keeps their concentration in scanning, zooming and feeling. Djokovic sometimes bounces the ball twenty three times before serving; Sharapova loosens up for her service with a standard repertoire of bouncing steps, and Nadal repeatedly tugs at his shorts. Drinking water or eating dextrose or a banana, besides providing necessary energy, may also be a ritual. Rituals provide a sense of security. All these routines instil self-assuredness, because they are always the same.

A few common rituals are adjusting an item of clothing or touching your cap, touching your nose or eyebrow, bouncing the ball, focusing on your racket strings or playing with them, and rotating the racket in your hand. They are a means of attaining or recovering the right mindset. If a player gets out of balance, rituals help him to recover his balance and rhythm, and to sustain that state. Most players have all kinds of rituals, but are not aware of them. They have developed in the course of their training over the years. Of course, it takes countless hours of training before the player starts using rituals 'unconsciously'. It is important to practise your rituals constantly, and always in the same way (that is what makes them rituals!). Rituals have to be unconscious actions that derive from routine. As soon as you become aware of your rituals, you shift to story thinking. If that happens, stop and wait for a few seconds and then start again, relying on your routine to get you through.

7. Eye control in between points

Eye control is an important instrument to ward off external influences. The player needs to be aware of what his eyes are doing in between points. If you are easily distracted by spectators, your opponent's behaviour, airplanes et cetera, eye control is indispensable. To keep your observation properly focused, zoom in on the strings of your racket, or your shoelaces, in between rallies. This will prevent you from being influenced by external events and improve your focus. This is so elementary, but it is one of the most important instruments that should always be used. It is very difficult to achieve action thinking without eye control.

8. Sound

If you have trouble suppressing your thoughts, sound can be a fantastic instrument to help shift you to action thinking. The sounds we refer to here are coming from outside. Concentrate on the sound of the strings when the ball hits it, and listen to the sound of your own breathing. Listen to the sound of your opponent's point of impact. This will help to prevent you from being distracted by external, irrelevant noises as well as helping you shift from thought to observation and feeling. Eye control and focusing on sounds are ways of using your senses to escape from story thinking. Often when players find themselves rooted to the spot in fear, the sound of their feet can bring them back to their body and start them moving again. This is a perfect example of using the concentration form feeling instead of thought. Sound is sensory, not rational.

9. Inner music

Many professional players listen to 'internal' music before and during their matches. It helps them to concentrate and to banish story thinking from their minds.

Inner music can help to suppress the judgmental, critical voice in your head, and it also serves as a way of achieving balance and rhythm. Music can calm you down and relax you, or quite the opposite, revitalize you and give you more energy. It is the most important 'last resort' if you are unable to escape from the claws of story thinking. The right song will transport you back to the feeling of action thinking straight away. Many players find it hard to appreciate that music can play a role during a match. But we believe that the reader can soon understand it by reflecting on his own life experience. Think of a party: whether or not you can get into the right mood may well depend on the music that is being played there. Bear in mind that music can help you to evoke whatever atmosphere you want on court at will, whenever you want. So you should realize that music can have a powerful influence on your mood. It can galvanize you or calm you down; it is a magic potion that is used far too little.

Having explained and discussed a variety of instruments that can help you escape from story thinking, we want to review a few of the points from the action thinking chart in chapter 3. We have taken these abstract points and shown how they relate to practical, tangible elements in your sport. By using instruments to bring about a change of concentration: beginning each action from feeling instead of thought.

Action thinking	Instruments / feeling / bodily awareness
now	rituals
relaxed	recovery time / breathing / heartbeat
presence	movement / sound
alert	trigger-words / eye control
realistic self-image	game plan corresponding to skills
self-development	short and long-term mental targets in training
calm	breathing
confidence	visualization / trigger-words
unconscious	breathing / inner music
being	rituals/ breathing / focus on action instead of the score / trying to perform as well as possible instead of winning

ASSIGNMENTS FOR INSTRUMENTS

To improve your concentration and to start each point with the right feeling, it is important to gain an understanding of how to use the instruments that have been described. Be aware of the fact that you can practice all of the instruments in every day life. You do not need to be in a training situation or match to work on the instruments.

1. a) Which of the nine instruments do you use most efficiently during a match?
    b) What benefit do you derive from it in terms of concentration?

    1. Trigger-words
    2. Visualization
    3. Breathing
    4. Movement and heartbeat
    5. Recovery
    6. Rituals
    7. Eye control
    8. Sounds
    9. Inner music

2 a) Which of the nine instruments do you use least?
   b) Can you explain why?

3 a) Which of the nine instruments do you consider that you neglect, and which should you use more often?
   b) How are you going to apply that in practice?

4 For the next 4 weeks, make a conscious decision to use at least one new instrument. Use your new instrument first during practice matches and training sessions. Pay attention to the affect that this has on your concentration. Work on it until it becomes automatic, and then use it to your advantage in match situations.

IMPROVING YOUR TECHNIQUE THROUGH FEELING

HOW CAN I TRAIN WITH CONSCIOUS COMPETENCE AND BODILY AWARENESS – ALL THE TIME?

To achieve technical progress, it is essential to base your training on feeling. One of the biggest mistakes that players make, in our opinion, is trying to improve their technique within a tensed-up play situation in which they all too often have to hit the ball with conscious incompetence, without feeling. If you work like that, it is almost impossible to achieve changes in your technique. That is one reason why some people may find tennis and other sports discouraging, full of techniques that are difficult to master.

Many experts mocked the father of the Williams sisters for playing very easy short balls to his daughters during training sessions that they could 'wallop for all they were worth'. Now that both sisters in turn have been the world number 1, it is impossible not to conclude that he succeeded in teaching them the 'right feeling'. He nourished their confidence by constantly allowing them to repeat something that felt right. Of course, players also have to be challenged by being pushed to their physical limits, but neglecting the regular training of the 'right feeling' will harm self-confidence. It is important for players to feel their own strength.

Why do most players get such a buzz out of drills in training? The coach (or ball machine) helps you by feeding you perfect balls. You don't need to do much yourself to create the right feeling and to train with conscious competence. This leaves all your mental energy free to focus on improving your technique. When used as a conscious aid, this method is obviously very useful. But it is frequently used as part of an unconscious consumerism, which leads to frustration as soon as the newly acquired stroke 'refuses to work' in a different training situation (e.g. a rally) or in a match, even though it was going perfectly during the training session with the coach. You can avoid this by learning a certain discipline in the way you train. Instead of acting like a consumer and having your coach drill you for hours, you can go out onto the court with a training partner, and practise what your coach has explained in a slow rally on a half-court (i.e. within the service lines). This half-court or 'mini' tennis enables you to base your training on feeling, and really ought to be appreciated more as a way of achieving progress in your game. Even professional players frequently introduce changes into their game by initially training in a half-court situation.

Example: woman, club player

Irma realizes that she has to learn to hit her balls with topspin to raise her game to a higher standard. With her flat forehand, she is making too many unforced errors. She goes to the court with her training partner and tries to apply her trainer's advice in practice. She has to modify her backswing a little to get under the ball ('dropping' the racket), which will enable her to hit the ball with topspin. In addition, her swing needs to be more relaxed to speed up the movement of the racket-face and increase its rotation. Her partner plays at roughly the same level, and the two of them are able to hit reasonable baseline rallies together. The problem at this level is that the flight of the ball is fairly irregular. The balls are sometimes high, sometimes low, and sometimes land some distance away from her. But Irma is a go-getter, and she is absolutely determined to get the hang of this topspin forehand. Unfortunately, without realizing it, her training oscillates between conscious and unconscious incompetence. Only when her partner plays her an ideal ball does she succeed in dropping the racket properly in a relaxed swing. But this only happens with one out of every seven balls. If the women had decided to start on a half-court instead, Irma could have achieved conscious competence far more often. Her partner would have been able to play the ball to her with greater precision (with a more consistent trajectory), and Irma would get the feel of the stroke far better, since she would be forced to perform it more slowly. At the same time, this kind of training improves concentration and would make it easier for her to base her play on feeling. The important thing is to stay in action thinking; if the play falters, it is because her thoughts have drifted into story thinking. The danger is that she will get bogged down in judging and analyzing the process, instead of playing from the feeling of action thinking. When learning, it is natural for your mind to be occupied with thoughts to begin with, but they should be the thoughts of action thinking: not judging, only observing. From thoughts you switch to feeling, even when training technique. That is the best way to achieve changes in your technique. It is best not to move back to practise the stroke from the baseline until it has 'become part of you'.

Example: man, advanced club player

George, an advanced player, wants to change his volley. He notices that when he goes to the net, he does not get under the ball well when hitting his first volley. His back knee is not close enough to the ground, which makes it impossible for him to get the right angle and hit the ball back deep and low. George asks his training partner to stand at the baseline while he goes to the net; he plays his approach shot and therefore believes that he is practising the first volley in exactly the right way each time. But he has failed to understand that this is precisely his problem. He is hitting the volley so fast that he is probably pretty much unaware of what his back leg is doing. He is training with conscious or even unconscious incompetence, whereas his aim should be to train with conscious competence.

If his training partner is willing to keep playing low volleys to him from the service line for five minutes at a time, George can practise with conscious competence, basing his play on feeling. This situation will enable George to train his action thinking. His concentration will be controlled by scanning, zooming and feeling, so that he will escape from story thinking, from 'too many thoughts'. The process of observation will be slower, enabling him to feel whether his back leg is in the right position or not. Only later, when the feeling has 'sunk in', does it make sense to move back and use the whole court; once that stage is reached, he can continue the training with conscious competence and eventually develop into unconscious competence.

CHAPTER 7

TACTICS ARE BASED ON FEELING

HOW DO I GO ABOUT FINDING THE RIGHT TACTICS?

This chapter clarifies the negative effect of 'thinking too much' about tactics. It provides a radically new approach to choosing the right tactics.

Here is a question we have asked a great many athletes: Can you remember any time at which you were making tactically good choices but were not in control of your emotions? The answer is always 'No'!

So what can a player do to improve his tactical choices? *Learn to attach more value to the instruments than to your thoughts.* Your emotions will then automatically become calmer and you will make better choices, from a clear state of mind. If we look at the graph of the Mindset bird again, we can get a deeper understanding of why emotions affect tactics. Imagine if one of the wings suddenly fails: the bird will take a nose dive.

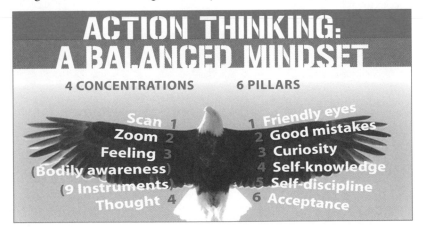

That is often the feeling a player gets when searching for the right tactics. If either the concentration or the pillars are neglected, the bird cannot fly.

In 2007, Robin Söderling played a quarter-final match against Rafael Nadal at Wimbledon. It turned into a five-setter and was played over a total of five days. Söderling eventually lost in the fifth set, by 7-5. Throughout virtually the entire match, Söderling had been irritated by what he saw as Nadal's 'time-wasting' and 'slowing down the pace'. He became so exasperated that he gave little imitations of the way Nadal pulled at his shorts during the match. It is not inconceivable that Söderling might have been able to win the match if he had not been bogged down in this story thinking. If he had converted this negative energy into action thinking (using instruments!), he might have been able to improve his concentration sufficiently to turn the match his way. Söderling's negative emotions left him far too little room to focus on the game. This must undoubtedly have influenced his decisions. His exasperation and mimicry deprived him of space to make the right tactical decisions.

The left side of the diagram below emphasizes the fact that Robin Söderling's thoughts in 2007 were taking up a great part of his energy.

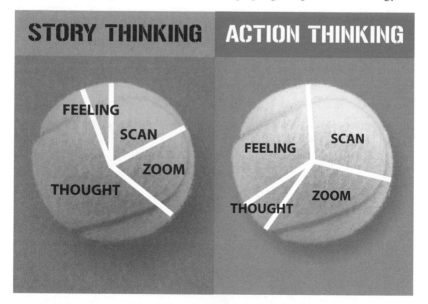

In 2009, in the fourth round of the French Open, Söderling found himself facing Nadal once again. His coach, Magnus Norman, had taught him what he should 'feel' in a variety of situations. In other words, he had taught him how to create the feeling of action thinking. Nadal was unbeaten in his last 31 matches on the gravel of Roland Garros. It was a unique record. But on this occasion he lost to Söderling, who played a brilliant match and revealed a completely different mentality than in the third round of Wimbledon in 2007. He showed his emotions after points that were well played, and covered his head with a towel at the changeover to keep out distractions and to stay with 'feelings' instead of 'thoughts'. His quick, light-footed movements in between the points kept him in action thinking (sustaining his heartbeat and agility). He displayed far more acceptance than in his match two years earlier, when his attention kept getting bogged down in irritations about Nadal. If you now look at the right side of the diagram, this represents Robin Söderling's concentration in 2009. You will notice that by diminishing our thoughts there is more space for scanning, zooming and feeling.

We often see similar things at the recreational level. A player with poor technique, who also moves around the court in a rather wooden and stiff way, finds himself playing an opponent with far superior technique who 'dances' round the court. After the warming-up, the better player thinks: 'someone with such a hopeless technique will be lucky to win any points from me at all, let alone a game.' When the weaker player hits all the balls back in the same fashion, without the slightest tactical insight, and the better player starts making unforced errors, the latter may lapse into story thinking. 'Surely I couldn't possibly lose from this bungling idiot?' Again and again he overhits his weak opponent's loopy balls, and... loses the match. His tactical instinct has become blocked, because he has been completely taken over by story thinking, judging instead of observing. Only by using instruments to produce the feeling of action thinking could he have banished the story thinking and turned the match around. If the player does not utilise his instruments, the mind wonders to thoughts and there is no time or energy remaining to find the best tactic based on the use of scanning and zooming.

Thoughts during matches

Are the following thoughts, generated by uncertainty and fear, familiar to you while playing a match?

- What am I actually doing here?
- Why am I doing this?
- Why is my strongest shot letting me down now, of all times?
- I know I'm going to make the same mistake again.
- I can't possibly win this.
- If I lose this match, I'm going to give up playing altogether.

Almost all sports people have thoughts like this on a regular basis. Negative emotions are deadly to finding the right tactics. That is because they focus on the perception of your own 'pain': for instance, your sense of unease because the play in a match is not going the way you had imagined. During matches, thoughts should be used only for the purpose of choosing clear, simple tactics. After that they must be disengaged to allow creativity and spontaneity to develop. The instruments of action thinking help to release you from thoughts and negative emotions and to lead you to the right feeling, the here and now of a match. They help to shift your attention from concern about your own unease, pain and frustrations to the visual alertness and creativity and courage that are needed to arrive at the right tactics.

It is difficult to differentiate clearly, in tactics, between zoom, scan, feeling and thought, but the following table will nonetheless be useful in clarifying the different mindsets: story thinking versus action thinking. It was written from the perspective of a recreational player, but the same points essentially apply to advanced competitors. NB. We assume here that advanced players recognize the points made and can translate them to their own level of play on the basis of their own experience. The focus here is on how to gain tactical insight through positive emotions. These emotions ensure that your attention shifts to scanning and zooming: the ball, the opponent, your own position and the opening in the court.

Comparing tactical insight of story thinking and action thinking

	Zoom	Scan	Feeling	Thought
Action thinking	I see that my opponent is attacking my short shots with his forehand. I immediately move back to gain time.	I see that my opponent is standing all the way over on the left of the court to exert constant pressure with his forehand on my backhand. I shall adopt the same position and see how he reacts to my change of position.	I feel that my opponent's first serve comes onto my racket face with great power; I do not allow it to rattle me, and keep moving through the ball, staying low. My trigger-words are 'low and through'.	During my 'thinking time' when changing ends (at the office), I realize that I have to attack my opponent's second serve. I visualize precisely where and how I shall hit the return.
Story thinking	I see that my opponent attacks my short shots with his forehand. Oh no! Where is he going to put it away this time?	I see that my opponent is standing all the way over on the left of the court to exert constant pressure with his forehand on my backhand. It's such an intimidating and irritating thing to do.	I feel that my opponent's first serve comes onto my racket face with great power; I get so rattled that I do not stay low long enough and jump up, as a result of which I keep missing the return.	During my 'thinking time' when changing ends, I realize that I have to attack my opponent's second serve. It gets me down, since I know it means I will have to take a lot of risks and I am afraid of making unforced mistakes

Discoveries triggered by Mindset training sessions

A variety of tactical approaches were tried out during the development of the Mindset method that we use in our training sessions. One of them, which produced some surprising results in relation to the 'malfunctioning machine', was as follows: one of the two players keeps consistently to a specific (undisclosed) game plan, while the opponent has to figure out what this plan is, in the course of a number of games. What struck us: in general, this exercise proved less beneficial than you would expect. True, those whose task it was to discover their opponent's 'secret pattern of play' learned to pay more attention to 'watching' their opponents' game and to recognizing patterns of play, but their own play often faltered as they did so. In situations in which the player would normally score a point, there tended to be more unforced errors than usual. The players were getting stuck in their thoughts! The same applied to those who had to keep rigidly to a specified game plan. Since they kept to this plan (in accordance with the assignment) they had to let certain opportunities (openings) in the game go, which stifled their creativity. As a result, they gravitated to story thinking. So while the exercise proved its usefulness, it had a big disadvantage. Both players concentration fell into story thinking.

What caused this? When the players were subsequently instructed not to figure out the agreed patterns of play but instead to focus on using the instruments that would enable them to shift to action thinking, the result was surprising. The players started observing what their opponents were doing better than normal, and saw through their opponents' pattern of play. They also took better, more creative decisions about what they wanted to do with the ball. What is the explanation? The solutions arose from the silence of action thinking instead of the noise of story thinking. By adhering rigidly to game patterns or being constantly absorbed in thoughts, trying to 'guess' the opponent's game plan, the players ended up in story thinking. When they used instruments to engage action thinking (visualization, breathing, eye control et cetera), they started to observe more clearly and to play far better than when following instructions to keep to a particular game plan or to compulsively focus on the opponent's game pattern.

Converting thoughts into feelings and observation is one of the hardest skills to master in all disciplines. Players struggle with it right up to the very highest level. Still, everyone can (and must) deal with it at his own level. The key factor is your willingness to work, one step at a time, on mental aspects of your game, to be flexible, and to change your mindset from story thinking into action thinking.

If you have noticed your opponent's weak points during warming-up, you can change your tactics if needs be. What matters is to exploit your opponent's weak points and to use your own strengths. Once you have mastered this, it becomes a fantastic cat-and-mouse game. anyone can achieve this, but the absolute prerequisites are creativity and courage.

What is creativity and courage?

Being creative and courageous means constantly being on the lookout for openings, even when something painful happens (losing a point). Instead of holding on stubbornly or 'withdrawing' into your game plan, you search for a new or modified tactic. Players are often reluctant to abandon the security of their game plan. If that is a conscious choice it may be a good decision, for instance to allow the game plan time to succeed. Unfortunately, however, people will often cling to it because they lack the creativity or courage to explore the unknown. The solution is often close at hand and fairly obvious, but the mental and physical energy required to change is crucial.

Sometimes you may try something out, but if it doesn't work in the rally, you feel unsettled. You need to preserve your flexibility and to try to react constantly on the basis of your observations.

The following two anecdotes illustrate the two opposite ways in which distracting thoughts may affect the player's creativity and courage.

Story-thinking club player

While changing ends, I think back on what a fantastic summer I've had up to now. I've won two tournaments! Club players are usually completely unable to cope with my high topspin balls. But now it looks like I'm going out in the first round! That woman can't even hit a decent forehand or backhand! One of those beanpoles that just rushes to the net all the time. She's so tall that she keeps managing to volley all my topspin balls. I'm really sick of it. It's just maddening the way she keeps on going to the net! I feel like I'm being besieged.

Action-thinking club player

While changing ends, I recall that club players are usually completely unable to cope with my topspin balls. But now I've encountered someone with a different type of game, who keeps going to the net and can handle them. She keeps on putting my high topspin balls away. I'll see if I can disrupt her volleys by hitting the ball lower over the net with even more topspin, so that the ball lands on her feet. Throwing in a few lobs now and then.

Creativity and courage means constantly searching for new ways with the right mindset. As the above anecdotes make clear, that is not always easy, but it is always better then making no change whatsoever.

How should I begin a match and when should I change my tactics?

You should start every match with a game plan. A game plan devised beforehand usually consists of patterns that are familiar to you and is based on exploiting your own strengths. When playing at a high level, both player and coach will have analyzed the opponent's game in detail. A specific game plan is chosen, one that is tailored to the specific opponent. But even without having any knowledge of your opponent, it would be sensible to decide on what tactics you want to employ before going onto court. The most advanced players start almost every match in the same way. They decide to apply certain familiar patterns of play. This generally means aiming for depth in their shots, mainly cross-court with topspin. This helps to develop a good match rhythm and to build up self-confidence. It avoids making unforced errors at the beginning of the match and helps the player to quickly get their strokes into the right rhythm. This is the best and easiest way to get rid of the initial match nerves. You don't modify your tactics until you are sure that they are not winning you enough points; in that case you adopt a new set of tactics, based on your opponent's game. For your tactics to succeed, your concentration has to be based on feeling, scanning and zooming, to be able to observe what exactly is happening during the match. To achieve this, it is essential to deploy 'instruments'. Players often fall into the trap of constantly trying to 'think' of a way to improve their situation in the match. This is internal concentration, which will detract from the external concentration you need. The body becomes stiff, and observation and anticipation become slower. As a result, you find yourself playing below your potential and not being able to choose the best suited tactic.

Why is it so difficult to change tactics?

It is difficult to change tactics because you assume you can win with the game plan you have thought up beforehand. You assume that you can play the match either with conscious competence (cc) or even with unconscious competence (uc). As the match progresses, you make what may be a disappointing discovery: that you have to change your tactics. It is necessary because your own game is not working (or not working well enough) and you end up playing with conscious incompetence (ci). That is often a painful realization. In everyday life you usually have enough time to think about problem situations and to find a solution. In sport you don't have that time; only very brief periods of time are available for such decisions.

Another reason why players find it so hard to change their tactics is a lack of interest in what is happening on the other side of the net. What the opponent does with the ball may sometimes lose you a great many points. Instead of allowing this to irritate or discourage you, it would be better to take a real interest in how these actions are succeeding. That is not always an easy thing to do.

Take an example that has nothing to do with tennis. Admittedly, this comparison may come across as rather far-fetched, but it may help you to define to yourself exactly what it is that is preventing you from acquiring tactical insight.

A good friend confronts you with the fact that he finds you unreliable. This hurts you. You might react in a variety of ways:

1. you feel hurt, do not react at all in the first instance, and withdraw into your shell;
2. you get angry and say that no one else has this opinion of you;
3. you ask your friend what this accusation is based on.

As we know, many people react in the first or second way. This is comparable to what may happen during a match. You take too little interest in the cause, but react instead to what it does to you. Reactions 1 and 2 can be classified as story thinking, while reaction 3 is action thinking. Being curious about your opponent's play (compared here to your friend's feeling) in a non-judgmental way and without allowing yourself to feel crushed by the disappointing result (compared here to the feedback provided by your friend) is a prerequisite for acquiring tactical insight. The pillar of curiosity is paramount.

Dealing with tactical changes in matches

You can think of your own version of the following examples for any sport. In a soccer match, say, the situation in which your team is first ahead by 1–0 and then falls behind at 1–2 would conjure up the same feelings as the tennis example given below. This match situation will sound familiar to many players.

You are 6-3, 2-1 up in the match, and suddenly your opponent changes his tactics. He increases his pace or suddenly keeps going to the net. The match turns around, and you lose the second set by 6-2. At moments like this, many players of all levels respond in one of the following ways.

1. You keep rigidly to your own game, while deep down you no longer believe in it.
2. Panic strikes, you don't know what tactics to adopt. So many possibilities present themselves that you can't see the broader picture and you desperately try out a ragbag of different tactics. You change your plan every two points and do not dare to rely on a steady tactical approach.
3. You choose a tactical approach that is beyond your capabilities. For instance, you start playing a service-volley game, even though it is not

in your 'suitcase'. Or you start hitting the ball even harder than your opponent.

4. You don't make any tactical choices at all and lose all control over your game. Even your original game plan is a distant memory. You move around the court in a complete daze.

We are not going to suggest all sorts of game patterns for specific situations here, these have already been discussed in plenty of highly expert, useful books by other authors. You will find our tactical answers to the situation described above based on mental changes.

The first simple but necessary support in changing tactics is the way you spend your time during a change-over (at the office). Here is an example of how you could divide your time up to achieve some inner calm when you have lost your way.

a. 30 seconds' relaxation (taking a drink and regulating your breathing)
b. 30 seconds' focused thought (make a simple decision)
c. 30 seconds' visualization (see in your mind's eye how you are going to apply your tactics)

Make your priority in the first thirty seconds relaxing. Have something to drink and allow your breathing to settle into a regular rhythm. Wipe off your sweat and sit down, relaxing your muscles. Then take no more then thirty seconds to think about the game you want to play and make a definite decision about the tactics you are going to use. Do you need to make any changes or not? By making yourself keep to the thirty seconds' time limit, you will make a decision quickly and simply. This will prevent you from getting stuck in your thoughts. Then use the next thirty seconds to visualize the tactics you want to apply.

Let's go back to the 6-3, 2-1 match situation on the previous page. What would be good decisions to make in your thirty seconds' thinking time when changing ends, at the office?

1. Suppose your opponent's stamina is only so-so. You know that he can't keep up his present tactics with its fast pace and going to the net all the time for very long. In this case, there is no need to change your game.

2. If it is clear that your opponent's stamina will enable him to sustain his change of tactics, you will have to change your own tactics too. One solution would be to play the balls (including the return of serve) high and deep, making it impossible for your opponent to keep to these tactics. The fact that this doesn't feel good does not necessarily mean it's not the right thing to do.

3. You go to the net more often yourself and try to seize the initiative. You do so full of courage and conviction, within the context of action thinking. You use your instruments to radiate self-confidence.

How long does it take to know if my tactic works?

A tactic has to be applied for about three games before you draw the conclusion that it isn't working. Give yourself enough time to get into the groove of your chosen tactics. That takes not only discipline and perseverance, but courage too. Take this example. You want to disrupt the game by varying the length of your balls, but every time you hit a short ball, your opponent scores. Instead of abandoning your tactic, you should first analyze exactly what is enabling your opponent to score (translate scanning and zooming into thought). Is it that your approach shots lack depth, so that your opponent is not far enough behind the baseline before you decide to hit your short ball, making it easy for him to get to your short ball quickly? Are your short balls too high? Are you placing your short balls poorly (through the middle of the court)? Do you keep hitting the short ball to your opponent's strongest side? You can't identify the reason why your tactics are failing until you have played a few games.

> Athletes need to realize that scanning and zooming provide the answers to thoughts, not the other way around.

What can help me to improve my use of tactics?

When Marcos Baghdatis told John McEnroe once in an interview that he had not decided beforehand on a game plan for a particular important match, many people were sceptical. A professional player without a game plan? But Baghdatis was being quite truthful. Professional players have so much experience that they can sometimes trust blindly to their intuition (feeling) so that the tactics unfold spontaneously in the rallies from zooming and scanning (external concentration). Baghdatis's comment indicates how important feeling is where tactics are concerned. We are obviously not trying to suggest that it is unimportant to analyze your opponent's game beforehand. We do maintain, however, that creativity and courage enables players to cope with changes in tactics more easily and effectively.

During a match, the rallies involve a constant interplay between tactics, feeling and observation. In between points, it is trigger-words, not thoughts, that play the most important role. If you drive yourself with brief trigger-words, your tactics will be far likelier to succeed than if you keep churning over long sequences of thoughts in your mind. Trigger-words like 'stay low', 'move forward', 'attack the backhand', 'change direction' or 'hit it deep' can help to produce the right concentration.

> Visualization and trigger-words are the best instruments for translating the 'chosen' tactics into action. They will help you to conquer the thoughts of story thinking.

1. Visualize the following two situations for about two minutes each:

   a. Everything is going well and you realize you are in a flow. Suddenly, because you start thinking, everything starts to slip away from you. How does that feel? What are the emotions that accompany it?

   b. Nothing is working and you're feeling desperate. What emotions accompany this situation? Can you conjure them up?

2. How many hours do you train tactical insight (practice matches) in relation to the time spent on training technical skills? Express the answer as a percentage. If this reveals a skewed ratio, you know what you need to do.

3. a. What are your usual tactics at the beginning of a match? Describe them, be specific.

   b. Do you have a 'game plan B' that you can revert to if your 'game plan A' tactics are unsuccessful? Describe it.

   c. In what respect would you like to improve your tactics, and how could you do so?

4. Do you remain 'curious' if your tactics do not work?

5. In what respect do you consider that you possess creativity and courage during a match? Give two examples.

6. Conjure up the above two situations again, and see yourself becoming calm using your favorite instruments and playing a strong tactical game.

If you practise assignment number 1 regularly, your emotions will have far less strong a hold on you when these situations crop up. They will have become more familiar and it will be easier for you to distance yourself from them. It's a fantastic discovery to realize that you can do this whenever and wherever you want. And it has so much added value. Raising your awareness in this way is the path of the action thinker.

PASSION

PUMPING YOURSELF UP OR LETTING IT OUT?

If a tyre is flat you have to pump it up, otherwise it's difficult to make any headway. But if you pump it up too hard, you have a bumpy ride and there is a risk of the tyre bursting. You have to allow a little air to escape. It is essential to keep the tyre under the right pressure. The pressure must not be too high or too low. Emotional balance works in exactly the same way.

There are three possible ways of using your emotions to induce or sustain action thinking:
1. Pumping yourself up
2. Release: letting it out
3. Inducing calm

It's important to learn to deal with your emotions and that you know how to use them at the right moments to achieve a sense of equilibrium and to play with the right passion. Sometimes you will need to pump yourself up: this can be done using words of encouragement or positive gestures that fire you up, like raising a clenched fist. On other occasions you may want to 'let out' the pressure (which will therefore reduce the pressure) by releasing your feelings with a strong verbal response, a real shout of emotion and an expressive gesture. Then there are other times when it is good to stay calm and keep your emotions stable.

Many sports people, even world-ranking players, have difficulty striking this balance. They often have to learn it by a process of trial and error. The important thing is to manage your emotions so as to cultivate the right amount of passion, which induces action thinking.

Until he was twenty-one, Roger Federer frequently lost his temper on court. He relates that one day, when he was twenty one years old, he simply decided that this had to stop; he didn't want to express his emotions in this negative way any more. He says that this led to a difficult 'searching' period, since he often felt that he was too quiet: he had a sense of 'floating around the court'. Now he has learned how to strike a balance between 'letting it out', 'pumping himself up' and calm, but he says that it took a long journey to get there.

Every player needs to be constantly trying to achieve this balance. There is not one player in the current top ten of the world rankings who does not use these three methods of emotional management to play their matches with passion. Pay attention to this, next time you're watching a match.

Amélie Mauresmo provides a perfect example. After beating Justine Hénin in the 2006 Wimbledon final (2-6, 6-3, 6-4) she said: 'When you are 6-2 down against Justine in the final of a grand slam you are not in such great position. You feel like, "OK, what do I need to do? Up until now I've been a bit shy. How am I going to change things around? How am I going to make it go my way? I really felt I pumped myself up. I let it out a little bit. I yelled a little bit. I was much more aggressive right from the beginning of that second set.'

This demonstrates that even top-ranking players are still involved in a constant quest for the ideal mental balance. Too much or too little 'letting it out', too little or too much 'pumping yourself up', too much or too little calm: any of these can lead to the player ending up in story thinking. Passion is an indispensable factor in sport, but even passion needs to be managed and kept within the right proportions.

Expressions of passion at different moments in a match:

1. *Release some pressure:* Release, let it out – jump in the air or shout a cry of victory after winning a tough point, and most importantly at key moments when you feel the match is turning in your favour. For instance: 'Allez!' is a shout that Federer uses lavishly at crucial moments in a match, with an appropriate gesture (often a jump). This moment of release will not go unnoticed by his opponent.

2. *Pump the tyre up:* Pumping yourself up: you feel yourself becoming a little passive, you encourage yourself when you feel your energy level sagging or after playing a good point by expressing something that reinvigorates you: for instance, you say 'Come on!' to yourself, raising a clenched fist or pumping your arm. This causes a release of adrenaline, a hormone that is essential to induce the best possible focus and to play with the necessary energy.

3. *Getting the tension right:* You know you're playing a good match; you choose not to express yourself, since you feel that the emotional tension is just right.

We would like to motivate coaches and players alike to make 'passion' a regular part of their program by training it in practice sessions. The more an athlete becomes aware of the power of 'passion' the more likely that he will be able to reproduce this in a match situation.

We suggest that you do three identical exercises for 5 minutes a time. Every 5 minutes you change the way you use your emotions after a played point:

1. you really let it out (so that the opponent can hear).
2. you pump yourself up.
3. you stay calm.

CHAPTER 8

ODYSSEUS AND THE LOTUS-EATERS

HOW CAN I GET INTO A FLOW?

Becoming conscious, one step at a time, of what it means to be in a 'flow', or the 'zone', and of how you can create the conditions needed to achieve it.

When the Trojan War finally comes to an end, Odysseus sets sail for his beloved Ithaca and his wife Penelope. It is to be a long and arduous journey, full of strange exploits and perils. When he and his crew come to the isle of the lotus-eaters (which scholars have identified as Jerba, an island off the coast of Tunisia) he sends scouts to check out the local population. The Greek scouts eat the unfamiliar lotus-flowers offered to them, which cause them to forget their homeland and to want to stay on the island. Their sole desire is to carry on eating the flowers and to bask in blissful oblivion. Odysseus has to use force to get them to leave and to continue their voyage.

Paradise or true happiness?

The lotus-eaters' paradise may sound like an attractive place to be, but does it really hold out the ultimate fulfilment that people desire? Is this fulfilment not simply a banal drug addiction that ultimately makes you into a zombie and keeps you in a crippling state of numbness and darkness? To achieve real fulfilment and happiness, Odysseus and his companions have to perform their task and can not allow themselves to succumb to the intoxication of pleasure. The psychologist Mihaly Csikszentmihalyi (pronounce 'chick-sent-me-high-ee'!) has demonstrated scientifically that human beings feel happiest not in a drugged-up state of lethargic well-being, but in a state of heightened alertness and clarity, which he calls 'flow'. Csikszentmihalyi describes flow as a state of complete absorption in an activity. At the same time, your skills are being tested to the utmost. The challenge of the task must be appropriate to the skill of the person performing it (challenge-skill balance, in Csikszentmihalyi's terms). If the task is too easy or too difficult, no flow can develop, he explains.

The purpose of Zen and other forms of meditation is to achieve this ideal alertness and clarity. And that is also exactly what we try to attain in sport. It is also called 'mindfulness': the elimination of past and future, and the total immersion in the here and now. In short, it means achieving total presence and complete awareness. The ego disappears, and a state of 'no mind' comes into being. People who never meditate will also recognize this feeling, from sport, music, work or cooking. You forget time completely, are utterly absorbed in what you are doing, and experience a 'buzz' of happiness. In sport, this feeling is usually called flow, or being in the zone. Both terms refer to the same state, one in which everything seems to be going automatically and you are working at the peak of your ability. Flow can't be willed or commanded into existence; you can't decide 'to spend some time in the zone'. What you can do, however, is to put in place the right conditions – the conditions that can enable you to end up 'in the zone', to experience flow during a match. This chapter is devoted to the subject of flow and the way in which these ideal conditions can be created.

Shameless consumerism

If not linked to a goal, the glorification of living in the here and now may lead to shameless consumerism. If Odysseus's scouts had carried on endlessly devouring lotus-flowers, it would not have made them happy in the end. Eventually they would have experienced a sense of frustration, as happens to drug addicts and alcoholics. In sport too, there is a consumerism that produces frustration. This point has already been raised (in chapter 1) in relation to the mindset of the 'malfunctioning machine' and in chapter 2 on the issue of consumerism versus investment.

Some players believe that putting in a certain number of hours on court automatically 'entitles' them to produce a good game. Others see sport skills as a product that can be purchased. They order some lessons from a coach and expect him or her to supply a ready-made product. Then, if they find that the product turns out to be defective, when playing a match, they take their 'malfunctioning machine' back to the 'shop' (i.e. the coach) to be mended. They fail to appreciate that to make progress in their game, they will also need to work on themselves. More importantly, they do not understand how exciting and rewarding this self-development can be.

Billie Jean King, six times Wimbledon champion between 1966 and 1975, said, 'I think self-awareness is probably the most important thing towards being a champion.'

It's your game! To a large extent, your fate is in your own hands. That so much depends on your own input is not frustrating; it is an exhilarating challenge. A good coach can provide guidance and help you on your way (see Intermezzo 2).

How can I get into a flow?

How you achieve the wonderful state of flow? It is a state in which everything goes automatically, as if body and mind have come together and you can trust wholly to the skills 'in your suitcase'. Story thinking is completely absent, and action thinking takes over completely. Chapters 5 and 6 discussed in detail the way in which you can achieve action thinking and the obstacles that need to be overcome. Feeling is the bridge you need to go from thought to the visual. For instance, you can use your own trigger-words as bridges to go from thought to the correct kind of alertness (external: scanning and zooming). Flow is only possible once you have achieved external concentration.

Bear in mind that you will not experience flow if you start thinking about it. You can't force it.

What are the conditions for getting into a flow?

Challenge

One important condition for achieving flow is that you have a big enough challenge; otherwise, boredom may set in. That is why it is so important to set yourself goals. Make sure that you always have a clear picture in your mind of your goals in a match or training session, goals that ensure that you are really challenged. Formulate a realistic challenge for yourself and focus all your attention on it. (If you find this difficult, ask your coach to help out). Luckily, in sport this is always possible. Even so, sportsmen and sportswomen often slip into a state in which it is extremely unlikely that they will ever get into the zone. There is nothing wrong with 'having some fun hitting the ball back and forth', but don't expect this ever to give you the euphoria that comes with the state of flow.

If you find yourself playing against a far weaker opponent, think up something that will help you to stay focused. For instance, hit every ball when it is still rising (upping the pace of the game), which forces you to move faster than normal. If your opponent is much stronger, set yourself realistic goals. For instance, try to win one point in each game by going to the net. You could then experience this as a victory.

Realistic self-image

The positive balance needed between challenge and skills can arise only if you have a realistic self-image. Take the following example. A player who loses his first-round match in a tournament to someone he judges to be 'inferior' to himself says afterwards: 'I'm never doing that again! Next time I'm signing up for a higher level; I just can't cope with all the messing about you get at this level!' This clearly belongs in the category of 'mentally unconscious incompetence'. Interestingly, you find even quite advanced players making comments like this. A player with such an unrealistic self-image is very unlikely to experience flow at the higher level envisaged; in fact it would probably result in even greater frustration. Instead, he or she should define a more appropriate challenge.

The personal success plan in chapter 9 will help you to formulate realistic goals.

The here and now

It is also important to remember that action and consciousness will only come together if you can switch off the 'thinking ego' of story thinking and operate wholly in the here and now. If you can do so, you will find yourself not thinking about your movements, but performing them effortlessly and 'automatically'. Earlier chapters have already discussed ways of escaping from story thinking and switching to action thinking.

Once you have achieved this, you have created conditions in which the state of flow can be experienced.

Winning or having the best possible experience?

Roger Federer has been very clear about this. He is not fixated on beating formidable opponents such as Rafael Nadal; what really matters to him is to be constantly improving his game. His role models include people like the golf champion Tiger Woods and Formula 1 racing driver Michael Schumacher. After taking his third US Open title, Federer said, 'I think that what people like Tiger and I are more interested in is not who we're playing against. It's wanting to get the best out of yourself.'

If your goal is to win a match and this win fails to materialize, the result is a sense of frustration. But if your goal is to perform as well as possible, you can still feel satisfied after losing a match, and even experience flow. The reason for this, of course, is that this mindset will help you get into the here and now; feeling that you 'must win' focuses your mind on the future, and therefore takes you away from action thinking. Flow can only be experienced in the here and now. Fear of losing will often hold you back: you will be risk-averse, and won't deploy your skills to the best of your ability. On the other end of the scale, complacency may mean that you stop challenging yourself, which blunts the alertness you need to perform well.

Letting your ego go

The main obstacle on the path to experiencing flow is your ego. The 'loss of ego' that occurs during flow is liberating, and may be compared to different forms of meditation. This experience can also teach us that it is evidently possible to live without the ego (to many people a terrible thought) and that this could actually produce a state of perfect well-being. It teaches us that by letting the ego go and engaging deeply with life, we can feel happy as well as achieving more. 'Letting go' is the key here; trying to impose solutions will impede the ability to experience flow. People who meditate, and who are familiar with this attempt to 'lose the ego', will have less difficulty letting go of their egos during a match, since the ego will not allow itself to be suppressed so easily. In fact the ego's most striking characteristic is precisely that it is always trying to expand, and will strongly repel any efforts to suppress it. The ego feeds on judgments and hostilities. These vanish in a state of flow. During a flow experience, actions are steered by the faculty of observation, not judgement. Any intervention by the ego will disturb that perfect chiming of action and consciousness. There is no place for the ego in action thinking.

What exactly is 'the ego'?

We have used the word 'ego' several times now, each time in rather negative terms. But what exactly do we mean by the word 'ego'? The ideas on the ego presented in this book have been distilled from our experiences with Buddhism. The ego is a complex concept – even within Buddhism – that is surrounded by many mysteries. Still, we do not believe it can be left out of consideration, since it plays an important role in our philosophy. How should the concept of the 'ego' be understood? How do we see it in relation to our ideas regarding the mental challenges of sport?

The ego is a mental construct from which we believe that we can derive our identity. It derives completely from a person's past and future. In the course of our lives, we form views, opinions, and judgements about others and about ourselves, and from this chaotic jumble we compose a picture, which we call our identity. The ego exists by virtue of its difference from other egos; difference is what gives the ego its raison d'être. Since it feeds on clarifying the differences with other egos, it is constantly setting boundaries and limits.

The ego lives on story thinking. In fact you could say that ego and story thinking are inseparable partners. Since the ego's biggest enemy is the here and now, and since the ego is wholly dependent on the past and the future, ego and flow are incompatible.

Relating this to sport, you might say that the ego shows its face most clearly in the thoughts of story thinking (*judgmental and hostile thoughts with which the ego identifies, irrational, negative and excessive thoughts*).

As soon as you allow the following points to sink in, the ego will lose its force and be replaced by unconscious and automatic responses.

> **Action thinking = loss of ego**
> 1 Thoughts from action thinking (thoughts arising from pure observation, without being attached to any judgment, short, purposeful focus on tactics);
> 2 Feeling through instruments (movement, rituals, breathing et cetera;
> 3 The visual (zooming and scanning).

Yoga

Many people find it hard to tell the difference between tense and relaxed muscles. Yoga can teach you. Yoga consists of techniques of switching back and forth between tension and relaxation – physical as well as mental – by means of breathing and physical exercises. Yoga teaches you to focus your energy constructively and to calm your story-thinking mind. Yoga also helps you to quickly become aware of the emotions that may take control of you – on and off court. Physical and breathing exercises can help you to quickly identify these emotions and determine what you want to do with them. Since you learn to recognize your physical limits better, you also learn to distinguish between different kinds of pain. Some teachers differentiate between 'green' and 'red' pain. Green pain is pain you should be aware of but that can be ignored (not denied). Red pain should sound an immediate alarm and generally warns you to stop playing immediately. Pain must never be denied since that causes stress. In the case of green pain in particular, you must relax. Yoga can teach you how to identify different kinds of pain.

There are many different kinds of yoga. Hatha yoga is the most common and popular kind in the Western world. It consists of physical exercises and techniques that foster breathing, balance, relaxation and concentration. The aim is to help you to feel more balanced and energized. An added advantage is that yoga improves the flexibility of your body.

Many prominent sportsmen have learned the benefits of yoga and now practise it regularly. When Ajax won the Champions League in 1995, the players started their training sessions with the yoga position known as the 'Sun salutation'. Their fitness coach Laszlo Jambor was well ahead of his times, introducing this technique into the rather traditional world of soccer.

Although meditation may seem far removed from sport, and even the opposite kind of activity, there are more similarities between them than you might think.

We have helped to teach players how to get rid of the noise in their heads using meditation and breathing exercises. It is far easier to experience a sense of inner tranquillity on a sports field when you have practised conjuring it up in this way.

Meditation is a perfect way of learning how not to identify with your thoughts or emotions. It teaches you that you have a choice: you do not have to be controlled by your thoughts or feelings, you can learn how to create mental space through which you can change your mindset. However difficult this may be, and however much practice it requires, it is possible to struggle free from the jumble of thoughts and emotions that seem to control you. For instance, suppose I do not dare to change my tactics. To speak in the terms of this book, it is possible to escape from story thinking and to shift to action thinking, as soon as you realize that you can choose not to identify with your thoughts or feelings. In our view, meditation is an ideal aid in achieving this. More and more prominent sports people use different kinds of meditation and yoga as part of their training. Raymond van Barneveld ('Barney'), five times World Darts Champion, practises Zen meditation for twenty minutes twice a day – three times in match periods. When he won his last world title, he said 'I am convinced that my new state of consciousness has helped me. I can meditate while standing on the stage. In the past, I was sometimes bursting with tension on the stage. Now I can play with my breathing.'

Everyone can devise their own methods of becoming totally focused at the start of a match. For instance, Billy Jean King used to stare at a tennis ball that was lying on the table in front of her for 30 minutes, without any distraction, before walking onto court.

Buddhist texts often refer to transformations of consciousness. There are many parallels between this idea and what we refer to here as a change of mindset, from story to action thinking. Read what Joseph Goldstein says about meditation in his book Insight Meditation, and see how easily this can be translated into our assertions about that mental switch.

'First of all we take a close look at this heart-mind to see what is what. Through the careful practice of looking, we develop a discriminating wisdom, so that we understand for ourselves what mental states are unskilful, that is, leading to suffering, and what states are skilful, leading to happiness.'

What is suffering? What is happiness? These are big words, but let's try to define answers that clarify the link with this book. Suffering arises when you identify too strongly with your thoughts and emotions, from the ego, from being judgmental, from story thinking. Happiness can be found in acceptance, letting go, selflessness, the now, non-judgmental observation, action thinking.

Meditation can help to transform story thinking into action thinking. Suffering will never disappear, but acceptance gives suffering a completely different feeling... the feeling of action thinking!

1. Have you ever experienced a flow? If so, describe it. If not, try and describe why, and how you could change this? Discuss this with your coach.

2. What does the statement, 'Winning from yourself is more important than winning from your opponent' mean precisely to you?

3. Do you think that the ego plays a role during matches? If so, what role does it play, and how do you plan to tackle it?

4. Do you mind losing? If so, why? Whose opinion matters most? Do you care on your own account, or do you care about the reaction of your friends, your team, your partner? Or for the recognition; the fame, the money, the glory?

5. Meditation exercise:
   a) Before the start of your next match, find a quiet place and look at a ball that is lying in front of you for twenty minutes (as noted above, Billie Jean King used to do this exercise for a whole 30 minutes before the start of an important match.)
   b) Then focus on your breathing for ten minutes. Breathe in and out through your nose. Do you notice a difference in the temperature of the air when breathing in and breathing out? If your thoughts are restless or you find it difficult, don't worry about it. Look at yourself with friendly eyes. The longer and more frequently you practise this exercise, the easier it will become to stop identifying with your thoughts.

If you come to feel that winning from yourself is more important than winning from your opponent, you will not suffer so much emotional distress from 'losing' a match and you will be able to leave the field with your head held high.

After answering these questions, you will be ready to start on your personal success plan (PSP) in the next chapter.

MINDSET AT ITS BEST

The 2008 Wimbledon men's final match between Roger Federer and Rafael Nadal set a new standard. Not just because the tennis itself was of an unprecedented standard of technical brilliance, but also, and more importantly, because we saw two players who could serve as examples to anyone in terms of mental resilience and sportsmanship. There was no petulant throwing of rackets, no swearing, and the opponents treated each other courteously at all times. In the speeches they made afterwards, both expressed their sincere admiration for the other.

The most striking thing was the extraordinary poise with which both men responded to the difficult points in the match. In the terms of this book, they displayed acceptance: they did not dwell on mistakes or questionable umpiring decisions, but played each individual point without allowing themselves to relapse into irritation or disappointment.

Their performance provides the living proof that acceptance does not mean hanging your head in resignation. On the contrary, it enables to ensure that your focus never slackens.

Nadal lost the third and fourth sets in the tie-break, which included the loss of two match points in the fourth set. When asked after the match how he had coped with these setbacks mentally, he used the word 'acceptance' twice, as if it was the most normal thing in the world. When the interviewer asked him if he had felt 'depressed' or that it was a nightmare and how he had dealt with this emotionally, he looked surprised and laughed. 'Why should I feel down? I am playing well; I accept that I lost two tie-breaks and lost two match points. I just have to keep fighting and keep a positive attitude.' In the fifth set there was not the slightest sign of any mental dip or reaction.

For this alone, he deserved the title.

STORY THINKING

ACTION THINKING

SCAN

Focused on:
- Opponent's position
- Opening in the court
- "Mirroring" your position in the court
- Surface of the court
- Weather conditions

ZOOM

Focused on:
- The ball
  spin, direction, height, speed, depth
- Opponent
  grip, shoulders, position of feet, angle of racket
- Coach/parent/partner for encouragement
- Opponent's body language (physical and emotional state)
- Racket strings

FEELING

1. Positive
2. Self-confident
3. Perseverant
4. Patient
5. With conviction
6. Motivated
7. Flexible
8. Courageous
9. Creative
10. Autonomous
11. Focused

INSTRUMENTS

1. Trigger-words
2. Visualization
3. Breathing
4. Movement & heartbeat
5. Recovery
6. Rituals
7. Eye control
8. Sound
9. Inner music

THOUGHT

Present
Non-judgmental
Observant
Tactics:
Clear and decisive

SCAN

Distracted by:
- Spectators
- Another court
- Moving objects other than the ball
- Difficult weather

ZOOM

Distracted by:
- Opponent: arrogant, irritating, overwhelming
- Clothes / rackets
- Coach / parent / spectators
- Facial expression; agressive, unfriendly, off-putting
- Body language: way of counting, swearing
- Opponent's comments
- Bad bounces

FEELING

1. Negative
2. Uncertain
3. Giving up
4. Impatient
5. Hesitant
6. Listless
7. Stubborn
8. Fearful
9. Predictable
10. Dependent
11. Distracted

INSTRUMENTS

1. Negative trigger-words
2. Haunting images
3. Rushed / irregular breath
4. Paralysed
5. Restless
6. Rushed or no rituals
7. Distracted eyes
8. Distracting sounds
9. Noise in your head

THOUGHT

Past and future
Judgmental
Hostile
Too many thoughts
Irrational

WHAT DO YOU CONCENTRATE ON?

148

MINDSET MINDMAP

STORY THINKING

www.themindset.eu

6 PILLARS

1 Friendly eyes
2 Good mistakes
3 Curiosity
4 Self-knowledge
5 Self-discipline
6 Acceptance

ACTION THINKING

9 INSTRUMENTS

Trigger words 1
Visualization 2
Breathing 3
Movement & heartbeat 4
Recovery 5
Rituals 6
Eye-control 7
Sound 8
Inner music 9

4 CONCENTRATIONS

FEELING
SCAN
ZOOM
THOUGHT

FEELING
SCAN
ZOOM
THOUGHT

STORY THINKING

STORY THINKING

STORY THINKING

Personal Success Plan

CHAPTER 9

PERSONAL SUCCESPLAN FOR ACTION THINKING (PSP)

THE ROAD TO TOP PERFORMANCE

While reading this book, you have answered various questions and done a number of exercises relating to the mental side of sport, based on the six pillars, four concentrations and nine instruments. Now you will be given the opportunity to define these parameters more sharply and to work on them individually. It is time to apply all of the Mindset method to become an action thinker.

Players of all levels constantly say: 'Yes, I understand what you mean about the influence of mental processes, but I just don't see how I can bring a change about.' Now you can put this to the test.

You will be training both wings of the bird – the pillars and the instruments – and by doing this you will learn to balance your mind.

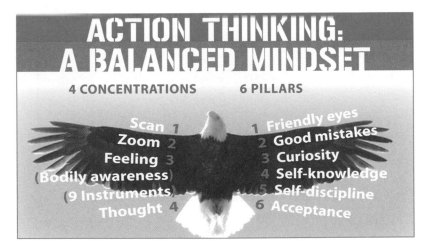

DEFINING A GOAL

How do you identify the goal best suited to you, to increase your mental resilience and to enhance your performance? You can do so by looking back at the assignments you have already carried out while reading this book. You are also advised to listen to feedback from your coach, fellow players or other people close to you when trying to define the right mental goal.

If you find it hard to think of something yourself, look back at the assignment for self-knowledge. Choose one of the characteristics of story thinking that you want to convert into action thinking. Choosing one of the six pillars as your mental goal might be an excellent way to begin.

Story thinking	1	2	3	4	5	Action thinking	1	2	3	4	5	
judgmental eyes						*friendly eyes*						
lazy mistakes						*good mistakes*						
indifference						*curiosity*						
ignorance						*self-knowledge*						6 Pillars
boredom						*self-discipline*						
complacency						*acceptance*						
negative						positive						
insecure						self-confident						
giving up						persevering						
impatient						patient						
full of doubt						with conviction						
apathetic						motivated						
stubborn						flexible						
fearful						courageous						
predictable						creative						
dependent						autonomous						
easily distracted						focused						

Later on in the chapter you will find some detailed examples of ways to put your plan for success into practice.

HOW DOES IT WORK?

1. **What do I want to achieve?** Start by deciding which aspect of your game you want to work on. Choose a single goal from the above chart or any other mental goal you want to achieve.

2. **What is holding me back?** Then define what is preventing you from achieving your goal, or has prevented you in the past. Also ask what people close to you think is holding you back.

3. **What do I stand to gain, in sport and in everyday life?** Write down what benefits you would derive from working on your chosen goal, both during matches and in everyday life. For example self confidence will be developed not only for your sport, but also as a person. The same counts for enjoyment and self respect. This is what you stand to gain. Be specific.

4. **How am I going to achieve this?**
   Then decide the specific way in which you want to achieve this. How do you go about this? With any goal, it is essential to always
   a. look at yourself with 'friendly eyes' and recognize 'good mistakes', during sport and in everyday life
   b. use a trigger-word. Write it down twice, then put it in your sports bag and stick it on your cellphone. Even when you do not train, it is important to use your trigger-word to remain aware of what you are trying to achieve. The same principle counts for the instruments. Train them every day. It only takes a couple of minutes, and it is fun.
   c. and/or d) the next step is to choose one or more instruments to structure your efforts to achieve the chosen goal.

Besides the trigger-words, you choose one or two of the following instruments to help you (see chapter 6):

1. Visualization
2. Breathing
3. Movement and heartbeat
4. Recovery
5. Rituals
6. Eye control
7. Sounds
8. Inner music

5. **Who encourages me, and when?**

Choose at least one person (your coach, a fellow player, a friend or parent et cetera) who will take on the task of encouraging you and checking your progress (always with friendly eyes!). If your commitment is not only to yourself but also involves someone else, you are twice as likely to keep to it. Instead of experiencing resistance around you, you will feel support. What is more, your development will benefit from the feedback. Agree a set time in the week when you speak to the person concerned.

6. **Chosen period of time**

Finally, you decide for how long you want to work on the basis of this plan: one, two or three months daily.

WHAT RESULTS CAN YOU EXPECT TO ACHIEVE?

If you keep notes on your success plan, the following description gives a good idea of the kind of progress you can expect to make.

Recreational: one month daily
Intermediate: two months daily
Professional: three months daily

1 month = raising awareness: you become conscious of your mental attitudes and of what is needed to progress. This happens gradually and fitfully.

2 months =   higher level of awareness: you will notice a real shift in your mental attitude, from story thinking to action thinking.

3 months =   the changes become 'second nature'; you start to adopt new mental patterns of action thinking as a natural part of your game.

HOW DID OTHERS DO?

We have extremely motivating results from many disciplines of how 'story thinkers' became 'action thinkers' after using the PSP diligently for three months.

Try it, it's fun! And let us know how you did: info@themindset.eu

Recreational:

'I am still amazed that I can concentrate so well. The PSP and exercises for scanning and zooming are so simple, yet very effective. I now have tools to continue on this path and keep improving. Finally I'm beginning to get some tactical insight. This has raised my enjoyment level both in matches and training. I now win matches that I always lost in the past.'

Intermediate

'I have always said that tennis is 50% technique and 50% mental – maybe my percentage is not quite correct, but that's how I see it. Strangely I have never even thought of training the mental side before. If I think about that it means that for years I have neglected 50% of my game. A whole new world has opened up for me and I am now enjoying working and improving both my technique and my mentality.'

Professional

'When playing international matches I always used to get annoyed by the crowd, supporting their countrymen (never me), always my opponent. It really upset me that they would clap at my mistakes and never for a good shot. Now, since I have been using the PSP I realise that I have a choice. Using friendly eyes I manage to take more distance from the situation and can change my focus to the things that do matter. Strange to think that within three months I really have managed to change my Mindset.'

EXAMPLE OF THE DAILY PERSONAL SUCCESS PLAN (PSP)

1. What do I want to achieve?

To be bolder and more daring at tense moments in matches.

2. What is holding me back?

The fear of making mistakes or of making the wrong decision. The tenser it gets, the more cautiously I start to play. I do so because making mistakes makes me feel like a loser.

3. What do I stand to gain, in sport and in everyday life?

Greater self-respect, the ability to take decisions at important moments, to play without holding back, to achieve better results in the long run and as a result to derive more enjoyment from the game.

4. How am I going to achieve this?

a. Look at myself with friendly eyes and recognize good mistakes. When I find myself facing a tense moment, the kind of moment at which I normally choke, and it happens again, I look at myself with friendly eyes and notice the good mistakes. I see that I am involved in a process of change, I am doing my best, there is no point constantly beating up on myself.

b. Trigger-words. AGGRESSIVE! and DARE! are trigger-words that will help to make me bolder and more daring.

c. Visualization: 20 minutes before the match I conjure up the emotions I experience when I don't play boldly and with daring. I learn to recognize them, and I allow other, positive emotions to take their place.

d. Breathing: 10 minutes before the match I practise being aware of my breath. I make sure I breathe deeply when I feel fear welling up at important moments, whether in a training session or in a match. [N.B. If you don't play every day, practise deep breathing once a day at home for 10 minutes, see chapter 6]

5. Who encourages me, and on which day?

My training partner, once a week after the Friday evening training session I ask him how he thinks I'm doing.

	Name:	Miriam Foster
	Week no./date:	1 – 7 september
	Chosen period of time:	Three months daily
	What do I want to achieve?	To play boldly and be more daring

	Mon	Tue	Wed	Thu	Fri	Sat	Sun
Friendly eyes and good mistakes in sport	5	Day off	4	Day off	4	2	Day off
Friendly eyes and good mistakes in everyday life	5	3	4	4	5	3	1
Triggerword(s): Aggressive and Dare	5	2	5	1	1	3	1
Instrument 1: Visualise	4	1	5	1	1	3	4
Instrument 2: Breathing	5	3	2	1	1	5	2
Who encourages me on which day? My training partner on Friday evenings					5		

What mental victory have you had this week in sport or in everyday life?
It was good and useful to brainstorm with my training partner about my
success plan. Normally I wouldn't discuss these things with anyone but
my coach. At the beginning it was a bit strange, but I noticed that the
feedback from my partner really gave me energy to follow through with
it. She said that she already noticed a difference in my attitude and my
approach to the game. That for me is definitely a victory and it helps me
realise that I am now paying my attention to the right things.

Notes: I lose my focus in the weekend. My best day is Monday, when I
tackle my assignment most purposefully. Next week I shall see if I can keep
it up for longer. On Thursday I completely forgot about my success plan, I
only realised this on Friday. I did not beat myself up about it, I'm only
human. I managed to carry on looking at myself with friendly eyes. In
the past I might have already given up, as I would have been very disap-
pointed with myself. I'm glad that's changing.

MAKE YOUR OWN PERSONAL SUCCESS PLAN NOW

Lay this book next to your bed so that it is easy to remember to fill it in. Review carefully points 1–3 of your success plan every morning so that your are aware of what you want to achieve. Grade yourself every evening from 1 to 5 (1 = unsuccessful 5 = 100% successful). Do not get down on yourself if you often score low. This will change with time.
Answer the following questions:

1. What do I want to achieve?

_____
_____
_____

2. What is holding me back?

_____
_____
_____

3. What do I stand to gain, in sport and in everyday life?

_____
_____
_____

4. How am I going to achieve this?
a. Look at yourself with friendly eyes and recognize good mistakes during sport and everyday life
b. My trigger-word(s) is/are

_____

I will stick my trigger-word(s) in my sport bag, on my cellphone and on

_____

c. My first instrument is:

_____

d. My second instrument is:

_____

5. Who encourages me, on which day?

_____

6. Chosen period of time:
❏ _Professional_: three months daily
❏ _Intermediate_: two months daily
❏ _Recreational_: one month daily

Name: _____

Week number / date: _____

What do I want to achieve? _____

Review carefully points 1–3 of your success plan every morning so that your are aware of what you want to achieve. Grade yourself every evening from 1 to 5 (1 = unsuccessful 5 = 100% successful)
NB Start by making a number of blank photocopies of this diary.

	Mon	Tue	Wed	Thu	Fri	Sat	Sun
Friendly eyes and good mistakes in sport							
Friendly eyes and good mistakes in everyday life							
Triggerword(s):							
Instrument 1:							
Instrument 2:							
Who encourages me on which day?							

What mental victory have you had this week in sport or in everyday life?

_____

_____

_____

Notes:

_____

_____

_____

EXAMPLES OF PSP'S

Detailed examples to show how the PSP could be used in practice. We shall start with the six pillars and then go onto other common mental challenges that a player could choose from. We believe that friendly eyes and good mistakes are always essential to achieving success.

PILLAR 1: FRIENDLY EYES

What do I want to achieve?

I would like to be able to play an important match without constantly judging myself and the opponent.

What is holding me back?

So many things seem to annoy me. I can't stand it if my opponent doesn't keep the score or tries to intimidate me. I also hate it when I don't play the way I have decided to. I really get furious with myself and often end up thinking that I'm just a total loser. I can't believe that after all the effort I've put in that I play SO BADLY.

What do I stand to gain, in sport and in everyday life?

If I were to judge myself and my opponent less it would produce a totally different feeling in myself and in my game. I'm convinced I would not only enjoy the game more, but that I would also have more energy to focus on the things that really matter. This would help me to play better and to be more positive.

How am I going to achieve this?

a. I shall see the match as a learning process. Winning is not the most important thing. I shall take the attitude that if I do my best, there is no such thing as failure.

b. My trigger-word is: friendly eyes.

c. The instrument I am going to use is inner music. My personal favourite in situations like this is 'Don't worry, be happy' by Bobby McFerrin. With that song in my head, there is no time to get caught up in negative emotions.

PILLAR 2: GOOD MISTAKES

What do I want to achieve?

I want to be able to give myself the freedom to work on my game, experiment with new techniques and tactics, so that I can develop into a stronger and better player in the long run.

What is holding me back?

I hate losing. I always want to win, and I just don't care what I do, or what it looks like, to achieve it. My emotions seem to take control of me and I make choices from which I derive no pleasure whatsoever. In the short run, this might help me win the match, but I know that it doesn't help in the long run... only how do I get my emotions under control?

What do I stand to gain, in sport and in everyday life?

I would have a totally different feeling if I could change this. I would be able to play with great motivation and ambition, knowing that even though I might miss a shot I would normally make, I will become better in the long run. My matches would become opportunities for learning instead of battlefields. I would acquire more self-respect and become a more confident player. My self-hate would change into acceptance and this would be a welcome change.

How am I going to achieve this?

a. Whenever I make mistakes during the game, provided I did what I intended to do, I see it as a 'good mistake'.

b. My trigger-word is: 'Good mistake'.

c. The instrument I am going to use is movement: by sustaining a high energy level and constantly adopting a positive posture, I will prevent myself from tensing up as a result of mistakes.

PILLAR 3: CURIOSITY

What do I want to achieve?
To become more open and show more curiosity. To be receptive to information provided by people around me whom I regard as 'experts' and whom I trust. To be willing to listen to other people's opinions. Not to simply carry on down the same familiar path.

What is holding me back?
I know exactly what I'm doing, I'm sure that my solutions are the best and I'm afraid that if I allow others to influence me too much, my game will suffer as a result. Plus I have to admit I don't much like hearing about the areas in which I am 'unconsciously incompetent', I find it too painful. And to tell the truth, I can be a bit stubborn.

What do I stand to gain, in sport and in everyday life?
It's possible that things that have never occurred to me might turn out to be really good ideas. I do realize, somewhere, that I would make more rapid progress if I could adopt a more open and flexible attitude. My coach and fellow-players would probably find me more pleasant if I were to take an interest in their opinion and I would feel less isolated. This would improve our cooperation and in the long term help to raise the level of my game.

How am I going to achieve this?
a. Look at myself with friendly eyes and recognize good mistakes. If I lapse into 'lack of interest' and the attitude that 'I'm always right', coax myself non-judgmentally and be pleased that I am now conscious of it. Learn to quickly recognize a 'good mistake'.
b. Think of a trigger-word that reminds me to focus on what matters: BE CURIOUS / BE OPEN / ASK QUESTIONS
c. Visualize a new, different self. A player who is busy building up a store of information, enabling him to get the best out of himself. Not someone who isolates himself and concentrates only on what he already knows.

PILLAR 4: SELF-KNOWLEDGE

What do I want to achieve?

To acquire more self-knowledge and understand why I do the things that I do, even though I sometimes notice afterwards that they're not the right decisions and that I derive no benefit from them whatsoever. I know that I need to be more realistic with my targets and realise that to do this I need a clearer picture of where I'm at.

What is holding me back?

To be honest, I just seem to keep doing the same old thing. Even though I know that my trainers are giving me good advice. I don't think I've ever taken the time to analyze how I really want to do things. I seem to be stuck in a rut. I'm so caught up in my routine and my own small world that I don't even think to step out of it. I seem to keep chosing the wrong targets, things that are too easy or too difficult for me. Probably because I don't have the right knowledge of myself.

What do I stand to gain, in sport and in everyday life?

I would be clearer about what I want to achieve and what is reasonable. I would be able to set clear targets for myself, for the short and longer term. This would enable me to train in a much more specific manner and would certainly lead to more enjoyment and progress than just blundering on as I am at the moment.

How am I going to achieve this?

a. Look at myself with friendly eyes and recognize good mistakes. I am going to stop withdrawing into a passive, depressed attitude. I will no longer be content to say, 'Oh well, it's just not working!' This remark indicates that I am investing too little in self-knowledge. I will ask my coaches feedback on a more regular basis.

b. My trigger-word is 'be honest!' to keep myself sharp both on and off court.

c. I shall visualize myself as someone who is eager to learn and who constantly sees new and realistic possibilities.

PILLAR 5: SELF-DISCIPLINE

What do I want to achieve?

I would love to keep the promises I make to myself and my coach. When I say that I am going to achieve a target, I will do everything within my ability to make it possible to bring about a positive change in my game and reach that target.

What is holding me back?

I have so often set targets for myself that haven't worked out that I just don't have the slightest belief that anything will change. I have lost the enthusiasm to persevere. To be honest, it's quite easy to give up. I'm used to giving up, and so many players around me do the same thing that it doesn't even make me feel so bad.

What do I stand to gain, in sport and in everyday life?

If I were to train and play with self-discipline each time, I know it would feel good. This would help me to grow more confident and there is no doubt that my game would improve. The people who invest time and effort in me and my game will be glad that they won't have to nag me anymore. I will develop a better relationship with them if I show that I'm always willing to give 100%.

How am I going to achieve this?

a. Look at myself with friendly eyes and recognize good mistakes. If I don't succeed straight away, I will not give up. Even if there are hic-cups at the beginning, I will persevere.

b. My trigger-word is 'you can do it', 'step by step' and 'self-discipline'.

c. I shall use rituals as my instrument. Building disciplined patterns into my behaviour in between the points will have a positive impact on my game. I will re-read the section on rituals in Chapter 6.

PILLAR 6: ACCEPTANCE

What do I want to achieve?

I would like to learn to accept things that are unavoidable and not to get so upset about them. It would be much better to use this energy for things that matter and that I can influence. I wish that I was not constantly being carried away by my emotions. Especially when I think that I get a bad call or when I think my opponent is trying to annoy me.

What is holding me back?

Even though I know it's pointless, it somehow seems to provide a sense of relief to cultivate my annoyances and to dwell on them. I am so used to emotions of this kind that I can hardly imagine energizing myself without them. I think I must need them.

What do I stand to gain, in sport and in everyday life?

I would be able to convert negative energy that does not provide any benefit into vigorous action geared towards achieving change and improvement. Acceptance would give me a freer feeling and help me to stop getting bogged down in irritations and instead to switch my attention quickly to things that matter. This would make me more focused and help me to achieve more. I would feel a far better sense of balance.

How am I going to achieve this?

a. Look at myself with friendly eyes and recognize good mistakes. I am going to stop blaming myself or feeling sorry for myself, and go on to something more constructive. I will also stop concerning myself with my opponents behaviour and my negative suspicions.

b. My trigger-word is 'accept it'.

c. The instrument I am going to use is my breathing between points and in the change-over. If I constantly focus on that when I start losing my temper, it would help me to calm my mind and make it easier to accept things the way they are. I will practice this daily to make it become a habit.

MORE EXAMPLES OF SPECIFIC MENTAL GOALS AND TRAINING IN A TARGETED WAY

REALISTIC GOALS

What do I want?

To learn to set realistic goals.

Sometimes I think that I can master a new stroke perfectly within a week, or that within a year I could teach myself to play like Federer! I know that this is not realistic, and yet I can't let these aspirations go. During matches I often think, 'If only someone could give me a golden tip right now, I could easily win!'

What is holding me back?

I can't stand the fact that I have still not mastered certain techniques. If I really think about this, I realize that I am controlled by my emotions. The aspirations I have are obviously ridiculous. I think it's time I started to see the humour of it. This will make it easier to set new, achievable goals.

What do I stand to gain, in sport and everyday life?

I will be rid of my frustrations at being unable to perform a particular stroke. I'll play with what I have in my suitcase. During matches I won't hope for magical solutions, I'll just work hard. This will induce mental calm and make it possible for me to achieve steady progress.

How am I going to achieve this?

a) By looking at myself with friendly eyes and recognizing good mistakes. If I notice that my goals are unrealistic, I'll just smile and carry on with what is feasible.

b) Think of a trigger-word for realistic expectations: KEEP IT SIMPLE

c) Listen to Michael Jackson's song 'Ease on down the road' in my head as my inner music, to keep me from straying off the realistic path and to induce the right 'feeling'.

FOCUS

What do I want?
To be more focused when I'm playing my sport.
To enhance my concentration so that I play to the best of my ability.

What is holding me back?
I am too easily distracted. I am always noticing too many things. I see everything around me and am unable to shut myself off from my surroundings. As a result I anticipate poorly and make the wrong tactical decisions. I also notice that I am constantly absorbed in thoughts and that I literally forget to look.

What do I stand to gain, in sport and everyday life?
Better anticipation, better timing and better tactical insight. This change will enable me to train and play with more motivation and enjoyment. I will get better results.

How am I going to achieve this?
Go through the tasks described in Chapter 5 again, to gain a better understanding of exactly what keeps distracting me.
a) Look at myself with friendly eyes and recognize good mistakes.
b) Think of trigger-words that will improve my focus: SCAN AND ZOOM.
c) Use eye control in between points. Look at my racket strings or shoelaces before the point is played, instead of drifting off.
d) Listen consciously to the sound of the ball on my strings as a variation on scan and zoom. This will also increase my focus enormously.

REALISTIC EXPECTATIONS

What do I want?
To have realistic expectations of myself.
To get a better idea of what I can really expect of myself. I notice that I sometimes have totally unrealistic ideas. For instance, that I 'must never lose from so-and-so'; or 'if I win that, I've made it'; or 'he/she is really unbeatable'.

What is holding me back?
I am constantly comparing myself to other players. In particular, I'm obsessed with how often they train, whether they have a good coach, and which players they have beaten. I'm constantly attaching importance to things that I know do not really matter, such as 'he beat so-and-so, which means that I could never beat him'.

What do I stand to gain, in sport and everyday life?
I would not constantly be turning over things in my head, absorbed in irrational and irrelevant ideas. This would make me a more balanced player. I would be able to play on the basis of my own strengths instead of always thinking about what is supposedly possible or impossible. This would certainly increase my enjoyment and create more inner calm. It would also improve my performance in the long run.

How am I going to achieve this?
a) Look at myself with friendly eyes and recognize good mistakes. If I lapse into 'story thinking' I won't immediately beat up on myself, but I'll try to regain focus.
b) Think of a trigger-word that reminds me to focus on realistic things: WINNING FROM MYSELF, BE REALISTIC.
c) Visualize a new, different self. A player who does his best, without bringing in all sorts of irrelevant things. I compare this to my present behaviour. I try to really feel how it will be when I'm concerned with winning from myself instead of worrying about all sorts of trivial details.
d) When I'm changing sides (at the office), I'll read my trigger-word and keep my attention focused on myself. Drink, rest, and dwell briefly on tactics. If expectations come to the surface, I know that I can let them go.

PERSEVERANCE

What do I want?
To carry on fighting to the end.
To radiate and feel a sense that I will never give up. Stand tall, regardless of the score. Not hang my head any more.

What is holding me back?
I see myself as a loser. If things are going badly, I have no idea what to do and I'm convinced that there is no point doing my best, since this is not working. I can't conjure up the energy to be physically or mentally present in the game.

What do I stand to gain, in sport and everyday life?
More self-respect, a better relationship with the rest of my team and my coach. Instead of feeling like a loser, I shall be left with a good feeling if I have given my best. In the long term this will also produce better results.

How am I going to achieve this?
a) Look at myself with friendly eyes and recognize good mistakes, even if this feels 'fake' to begin with.
b) Think of a trigger-word that reminds me to persevere:
POISE / STAND TALL YES I CAN
c) Listen to Rocky's song 'The eye of the tiger' in my head as my inner music, to induce the right 'feeling'.
d) Keep my movement around the court and my heartbeat at a constant 'alert' pace, to be sure that I am physically present. Use a heart rate monitor to become more conscious of this.
e) Walk briskly with my head held high in between points, regardless of the score.

PATIENCE

What do I want?
To be patient.
To acquire more patience and inner calm during play, especially when things get 'difficult'.

What is holding me back?
I get impatient if it takes too long, I want to score straight away and get irritated if it doesn't work. Especially if I'm playing against someone who slows the game down. I start to rush things more and more.

What do I stand to gain, in sport and everyday life?
I shall make fewer unforced errors and take better decisions. Making the right choices at the right times will boost my self-confidence. I shall no longer lose from myself, only perhaps from my opponent. That will feel different; I will acquire more self-respect.

How am I going to achieve this?
a) Look at myself with friendly eyes and recognize good mistakes.
b) Think of a trigger-word that reminds me to be patient:
RIGHT CHOICES / KEEP IT UP / PATIENCE
c) During recovery, deliberately take more time to achieve inner calm, so as to avoid rushing into the next point.
d) Start using consistent rituals before playing a point to stop myself rushing things and to induce in myself 'a feeling of patience'.

AUTONOMY

What do I want?
To take charge of my game.
To focus on what matters. Not to allow myself to be influenced by external impressions any more, such as the behaviour of my opponent or of spectators.

What is holding me back?
I always see everything! My coach, the spectators, I tend to be easily intimidated by my opponent (his hard strokes or massive physique), other people shouting and making comments. My focus is never totally on the game, I'm always thinking of what others are doing.

What do I stand to gain, in sport and everyday life?
I would function with a totally different feeling, as a better and stronger person, and a better and stronger player. It would be wonderful to feel completely 'in charge' without allowing anything to influence me. This would undoubtedly raise the level of my game and lead to better results in the long run.

How am I going to achieve this?
a) Look at myself with friendly eyes and recognize good mistakes.
b) Think of a trigger-word that reminds me to stay focused on what matters: BE IN THE GAME.
c) Use eye control in between points, so that my eyes cannot wander off to the side or towards my opponent. This will make it easier for me to ward off external influences.
d) When changing ends (touching base) I'll read my trigger-word and stay focused on myself. Drink, rest and dwell briefly on tactics. I won't look around me.

A STORY TO END WITH

STRUGGLE

Once upon a time, there was a celebrated sportsman who lived in a remote kingdom. He never had to make the slightest effort. He did not have to train for hours to strengthen his body and his mind. He did not have to repeat the same monotonous exercises every day. He did not have to slave away at improving his skills, since they had been perfect from the outset.

In matches, his supremacy was so awesome that his opponents never got under his skin or needled him, or roused him to greater achievements. But since he always won with ease, he never experienced the pleasure of a duel or a hard-fought victory, the pleasure of coming from behind to win, or the joy of physical and mental satisfaction after a struggle.

– Bob Mitchell: *The Tao of Sport*

We believe that those who apply the ideas explained in *Mindset* will frequently experience the joy of physical and mental satisfaction. Buddhists sometimes refer to the 'ten thousand joys and ten thousand sorrows' that life has in store for us. If we have become familiar with the ten thousand joys and the ten thousand sorrows of taking part in sport by acquiring greater self-knowledge, this will open up the path to acceptance and the pursuit of realistic goals. Only then shall we have laid the foundations for a well-balanced and relaxed pursuit of sport. And then we shall be able to enjoy the sport we practise to the full.

My life has always been closely bound up with tennis, which I started playing when I was eight years old. I grew up in Weybridge, in England, and from the age of 12 to 16 I regularly represented England in international events.

On the tennis court I always had enormous problems with my emotions, over which I had absolutely no control. My last match in England was at the Junior Wimbledon tournament, where I got as far as the last sixteen. During that match I lost my self-control and accused both the linesman and the umpire of bad calls. Besides losing the match, I was quite rightly given a three-month suspension by the LTA.

Immediately after this I went abroad, harbouring grand plans to conquer the professional tennis circuit, without a coach and without any sponsors. I soon realized that there were problems in my game, and from 16 to 21 years of age I led a wandering existence as a semi-professional player. When I didn't win, I had no money for food or lodgings. So understandably, I was always fixated on winning. I was totally unable to cope with losing a match, so my tennis career produced a constant roller-coaster sensation.

In this period I managed to secure a scholarship for the Pepperdine University in Malibu, California, where I stayed for two terms, playing for the tennis team. But I couldn't settle in there.

When I started playing competition for a club in the Netherlands, in 1983, it felt as if I had come home. The freedom and tolerance was such a breath of fresh air! Amsterdam was the perfect place for me to settle down.

I worked for the Dutch National Lawn Tennis Association for a few years, as a district coach for young players who were hoping to turn professional, before deciding to start up my own business. I founded PTI-tennisreizen in 1991. The aim of PTI (=Professional Tennis Institute) was to offer one-week holiday training courses for club players and treat them in the same way as you would treat professional players. These courses gave me a lot of useful feedback from people from all walks of life, and I gradually came to understand that your attitude of mind on the tennis court was no different from your attitude of mind in life. I also discovered that the emotions of club players were often just as intense as those of world-class players.

The conclusion that attitudes can be learned started to grow during a sabbatical year and an extended period of travel in 2002. I had hoped that this trip would put an end to the inner turmoil and fight with myself, but in fact I discovered that the agitation in my mind kept getting worse.

After nine months of this, I decided to attack the problem once and for all. In Tasmania I surfed the internet in search of meditation courses. Since I could not find the rest I needed from any external source, I would have to look for it within. I discovered a strange site: www.dhamma.org. It provided information about courses teaching 'insight meditation / Vipassana' that were given worldwide, and they were free! My immediate thought was that it must be some sect or other. Getting up at 4 a.m., meditating for ten hours a day, no talking for 10 days, no writing and no seeking eye contact. But with time on our hands and nothing to lose, Jacko (my wife) and I decided to enrol for the course in the north of New Zealand.

That was the beginning of inner calm and new discoveries, and it set my life on a new course. One of the most amazing things I realized was that all the misery that plays out during matches is simply a reflection of what is happening inside you. If you are constantly focused on winning, it arouses feelings of tension, self-loathing and dissatisfaction. I finally realized why my emotions were uncontrollable and why I often tensed up at big moments. Because winning is not a goal. But constant self-improvement, along with acceptance and letting go, can produce mental tranquillity, as a result of which 'winning' actually comes within reach. Above all, winning from yourself. I also finally understood why the emotions on the court were so intense: you can't hide anything, you are exposed, everyone can see you. During my career as a coach, I have always been searching for an answer to this question: is it possible to practise sport at the highest level, to make a supreme effort time and time again, and to still be a balanced person who takes an interest in the outside world? I now believe it is.

After this experience, I wanted to start applying a new method in my PTI-tennis courses. I began to give training sessions based on what I had learnt about mindfulness in the Vipassana training course. We started emphasizing the mental side of training in the tennis trips. And then, during a tennis trip in Jerba, Tunisia in March 2005, the writer Hans Dekkers crossed my path. A miracle.

When we got back to Amsterdam, he conceived the idea of collaborating on a book about the 'PTI method'. He basically forged my story and his into one whole. The concepts of story thinking and action thinking come from Hans. He knows an enormous amount about inner struggles, and succeeded in presenting the philosophical side of the PTI method in an excellent, solid narrative. Without any doubt, my working relationship with Hans has been the best period in my career up to now. He inspires me with his ideas and his writing. I am enormously grateful to him.

Finally, I hope that the reader will now find it a little easier to negotiate all the obstacles that make sport and life such a challenge. Thanks to Eastern knowledge, I have learnt that climbing a mountain is just as valuable as standing on top of the mountain and looking out at the world with an open mind or running down the mountain with the wind behind you, experiencing the sensation of flow. Acceptance and surrender have far more to offer than wanting to win.

EPILOGUE BY HANS DEKKERS

Writing is a solitary activity, which some people believe is of no use to society at all. It can touch and move people, set them thinking or entertain them, but it can't usually get them to change their behaviour. So I consider it a great privilege that, as co-author of Mindset, I may contribute to a change of mentality in sport, and perhaps a change even wider-ranging than that. For me as the author of novels and poems, my period of intense collaboration with Jackie has been a totally different kind of writing: expressing a vision and a method that came out of the cooperative relationship itself. Creating a common 'mindset' in this way proved to be liberating, and produced an incredible flow.

In 2005 I booked a tennis trip to the island of Jerba in Tunisia, organized by Jackie. It surprised me not only that she was able to give the participants so much enjoyment, but more importantly that I started to look differently at my life. It became clear to me that Jackie approached her great passion, tennis, from a Buddhist perspective. In spite of my initial scepticism, I soon saw the practical effects of this approach. Without any woolly language, Jackie showed us the importance of the mental side of tennis and explained how you can work on improving it. I learnt that there are other ways of reacting to disappointment besides with anger and frustration, not just in tennis but in everyday life too. In addition, meditation created periods of tranquillity in hectic periods and I learnt to live more in the 'now'.

I felt that Jackie should do more with her unique approach. After that Jerba trip, I suggested writing a book about her ideas. That plan led to our collaborative venture. Her great expertise and experience as a coach and my own views as a recreational player and experience as a writer turned out to complement each other perfectly.

Martina Navratilova once said: *'Tennis has given me soul'*. I have never heard Jackie say that, but I felt it in every conversation we had.

Hans Dekkers is a writer. He has published novels, a collection of short stories and a collection of poems. He has also written for the stage and contributed to a number of literary journals. For more information, please see his website, www.hansdekkers.org

ACKNOWLEDGEMENTS

To start with, we want to thank our partners, Jacko van Meyel and Stasja Draisma, who heard the Mindset train thundering by almost every day and were frequently asked to jump on board. Without them, Mindset would never have materialized at all.

Also, a very special thank you to Stanley Franker, my (Jackie's) former boss when I worked for the Federation. Over the years he has always kept inspiring, motivating and challenging me. I admire Stan especially for three reasons; his honesty, his self-discipline and his kindness. I have used him as my example for how a coach should behave.

We received vital feedback and inspiration from Nora Blom, Roel van Veen, Frank van Fraayenhoven, Rohan Goetzke, Hugo Ekker, Annette Veth, Martin Koek, Jo Caris, Marion Spierenburg, Hesterine de Reus, Pons Jan Vermeer, Marcel Crok, Anke Reints and Hrvoje Zmajic.

We should also like to thank the following people for their special support: Jessica Dekkers, Janine Toussaint, Carla Siebenga, Tom Karsten, Niels van der Meulen, Pjotr van Dalfsen, Gido Vermeulen, Tom Kleijwegt, Franck de Beauvais, Johan Bolhuis, Bart Meijer, Joke van Klink, Janneke Hofman, Marco van Berkel and all the dedicated coaches and participants of 'PTI-tennisreizen' and Mindset training sessions.

In our international venture we would like to express our deepest gratitude to Aart Jan Bergshoeff, our graphic designer and co-worker. He has helped us beyond recognition with the official publication of the English Mindset. With patience, creativity and endless passion he has stood by our side and brought his talent into our team effort.

We are very grateful to Beverley Jackson for her terrific translation, her great sense of humour and her passionate involvement in the Mindset project.

Also we very much appreciate the generous quotes given to us by various top coaches, professional athletes and specialists.

Finally, we are indebted to Tirion, our first publishers, who helped us enormously by bringing *Mindset* onto the Dutch market. Aernoud Oosterholt and Roel van Veen were very generous with their support and insights.

RECOMMENDED READING

The work of S.N. Goenka (www.dhamma.org)

William Hart, *The art of living*. Harper. San Francisco, 1987

Stephen R. Covey, *The Seven Habits of Highly Effective People*. Simon & Schuster. New York, 1999

Eckhart Tolle, *The Power of Now*. New World Library. USA, 1999

Joseph Goldstein, *Insight Meditation*. Shambhala Publications, Inc. Boston, Massachusetts, 1993

Jim Loehr and Tony Schwartz, *The Power of Full Engagement*. Free Press Paperbacks. New York, 2003

Dan Millman, *The Inner Athlete*. Stillpoint publishing. New Hampshire, U.S.A., 1994

B.K.S. Iyengar, *Light on Yoga*. Schocken Books. New York, 1966

W. Timothy Gallway, *The Inner Game of Tennis*. Random House. New York, 1974

John F. Murray, *Smart Tennis*. Jossey-Bass. San Francisco, 1999

John Douillard, *Body, Mind and Sport*. Three Rivers Press. New York, U.S.A., 1994

INDEX

acceptance 17, 30, 37, 42–44, 63, 76, 80, 82–83, 147, 165, 173
action thinking 7–15, 21–24, 28, 41, 44, 52, 59, 85, 102, 119, 123
Allais, Alphonse 58
Andrews, Julie 42
anticipation 94
attachment to points 62
attention control. *See* concentration
at the office (change-over) 96, 129, 168
automaticity 103
autonomy 171
Baghdatis, Marcos 112, 130–131
Bargh, John 103
Barneveld, Raymond van 144
Basten, Marco van 57–58
battlefield or playing field? 19, 27, 60
bodily awareness. *See* feeling
boredom 41, 43
Borg, Björn 73, 88
breathing 13, 14, 59, 66, 92, 101, 108–110, 143
Buddhism 109, 142, 144–145, 173, 177
calm 134–136
challenge-skill balance 138
cheating 68–70
choking 13, 58, 63
coach 54–56
complacency 41–43

concentration 18, 85–99, 101
Confucius 37
Connors, Jimmy 73
consumerism 8, 28, 39–42, 116, 138
contents of your suitcase 43
Copernicus 21
courage 125–126
Covey, Stephen R. 9
creativity 125–126
Csikszentmihalyi, Mihaly 137–138
curiosity 16, 37–43, 50–51, 162
Dasayev, Rinat 58
dealing with bad calls 68, 70–72
Dementieva, Elena 105
discouragement 26, 77
Djokovic, Novak 112
ego 11, 59, 63, 138, 140–142
emotional balance 134–136
eye control 101, 113
failure 20
fear 8, 26, 38, 57, 60, 73, 77, 85, 102, 106, 110, 113, 122, 141, 156
Federer, Roger 11, 13–14, 30, 37, 85, 105, 135–136, 141, 147
feeling 9, 13–14, 18, 69, 86–88, 92–99, 101–102, 116–118, 119, 123
fists 105, 134
flow 8, 11, 60, 137–145
focus. *See also* concentration

four concentrations 18, 85–98
friendly eyes 15, 24–26, 30–31, 41–42, 160
frustration 28, 37, 59, 74, 102, 104, 116
Goenka, S.N. 9
Goldstein, Joseph 144
good mistakes 16, 25–26, 32–33, 41–42, 61, 78, 161
Graf, Steffi 111
heartbeat 101, 110–111
Henin, Justine 104, 135
here and now 11, 60, 62, 69, 86, 105–106, 109, 122, 138, 140–142
Hermans, Willem Frederik 58
hostile eyes 41–42
ignorance 41, 43
impatience 77
indifference 41, 43
inner music 101, 114
instinct 8
instruments 13–14, 101, 114–115
interdependance 54
investment 8, 39–42, 44, 138
irritation 32, 63, 76, 121, 147, 165
Ivanovic, Ana 104–105
Jackson, Michael 166
Jambor, Laszlo 143
Jankovic, Jelena 64
judgmental 24, 30, 41–42, 76, 98, 142
Jung, Carl 23

King, Billie Jean 139, 144
lazy mistakes 41–42
letting go 63–64, 141
letting it out 134–136
Loehr, Jim 9
malfunctioning machine 19,
    21–23, 57, 62, 101, 123,
    138–139
mantras 105
Materazzi, Marco 24, 69
Mauresmo, Amélie 135
McEnroe, John 73, 130
McFerrin, Bobby 160
meditation 60, 105, 109, 112,
    138, 144–145, 175
mental warming-up 34–35
mindfulness 11, 19, 21–23, 57,
    62, 101, 175
Mindset Mindmap 15, 149
Mitchell, Bob 173
movement 101, 110–111
Mühren, Arnold 58
Murray, Andy 98
Nadal, Rafael 105, 111–112,
    120–121, 141, 147
Navratilova, Martina 98,
    106, 177
Nideffer, Robert 8, 86
non-judgmental 16, 60,
    78–79, 128
Norman, Magnus 121
notes 105
Odysseus 137
over-concentration 85, 98
passion 134–136
patience 170
Penelope 137
perseverence 169
pranayama 66, 108–110
priming 103
pumping yourself up
    134–136
rationalizing 62
realistic expectations 168
realistic goals 166
realistic self-image 140
recovery 101, 111–112
respect 44–45
rituals 101, 112–113
Rocky 169

Roddick, Andy 105
Sampras, Pete 11, 105
scan 18, 86–99, 102, 123
Schumacher, Michael 11, 141
Schwartz, Tony 9
Seles, Monica 97
self-discipline 17, 41–43,
    61–62, 66–67, 164
self-knowledge 17, 22, 28, 37,
    41–44, 52–53, 78, 163
Shadow, the 23
Sharapova, Maria 112
six pillars 15, 18
Söderling, Robin 120–121
sound 101, 113
sportsmanship 105, 147
stages of learning 45–48
- Conscious Competence
    45–48, 116–118, 127
- Conscious Incompetence
    23, 45–48, 78–79,
    116–118, 127
- Unconscious Competence
    45–48, 127
- Unconscious Incompetence
    23, 45–48, 77, 79, 117–119,
    140
story thinking 7–9, 11–13,
    21–23, 27–28, 41, 43,
    57–59, 68–69, 97,
    101–102, 123
stubbornness 28, 59, 77
tactics 119–131
thought 18, 86, 89, 92–99,
    102, 122–123
Tolle, Eckhart 9
total alertness 60
total presence 60
trigger-words 13–14, 28, 35,
    59, 79–80, 101, 103–105,
    131
uncertainty 24
unrealistic self-image 76,
    140
Vipassana 9, 175
visualization 14, 57, 59, 60,
    62, 92, 101, 106–109, 131
Vriesekoop, Bettine 13
Williams, Richard 116
Williams, Venus 64

winning from yourself
    11–12, 80
Woods, Tiger 11, 141
Yoga 143
Zidane, Zinédine 24, 68
zoom 18, 35, 86–99, 102, 123

NOTES